DETOUR TO
DEATH ROW

By David Atwood, Founder
Texas Coalition to Abolish the Death Penalty

Published in 2008 by peaceCENTER Books
1443 S. St. Mary's San Antonio, TX 78210
210.224.HOPE   www.salsa.net/peace/ebooks
pcebooks@yahoo.com

ISBN 1438277733
EAN-13 9781438277738

Copyright © 2008, David Atwood. All Rights Reserved.

Dedication

To my wife, Priscilla, and my children,
Chris, Richard, Kathleen, Jennifer,
Michael and Joseph, who have stood by
me through this detour to death row.

Advance Praise for **Detour to Death Row**

"Dave Atwood's *Detour to Death Row* is an incredible journey which shows what can happen to a person who allows God to enter his life and lead him on different path. Who would have thought that an engineer working for an oil company would one day be leading the fight to abolish the death penalty in the state which leads the nation in executions? Dave's story is an inspiration to me, personally, and to anyone who believes in the sanctity of all human life."

> **Sister Helen Prejean, CSJ**, author of *Dead Man Walking* (Random House, 1993) and *The Death of Innocents: An Eyewitness Account of Wrongful Executions* (Random House, 2004)

"Dave Atwood is a dedicated advocate for human rights who has worked tirelessly against the death penalty for many years. This work is particularly difficult in Texas where officials strongly support capital punishment. Dave's book is a wonderful description of how he grew into this work and organized efforts in Texas to oppose this inhumane form of punishment. I highly recommend it to anyone who is interested in creating a more civilized society."

> **Frances (Sissy) Farenthold**, Texas legislator, attorney and educator

"David Atwood is one of those rare human beings who do their best to be human: never focused on himself, ironic, mild, a believer of human life and human dignity under any circumstance. He walks in the footsteps of Martin Luther King Jr., Dorothy Day and other great American peacemakers to help us discover a humanity without revenge and brutality and to use forgiveness and compassion to heal the wounds of the victims, ourselves and our society. David takes us on a pilgrimage from Hell to Paradise in a small Dante's Comedy, a journey to death row where we hear astonishing stories and meet incredible human beings. Texans — and all of us — must be grateful to this man who never gives up the dream and the hard work of helping a reluctant society reject the old, primitive law of 'an eye for an eye, a tooth for a tooth.' "

> **Mario Marazziti**, spokesperson for the Community of Sant'Egidio and co-founder of the World Coalition Against the Death Penalty

"A fascinating narrative of the journey of David Atwood, a stubborn oil company engineer, who decided to take on the State of Texas and its death penalty law, successfully putting the national and international spotlight on Texas' Killing Machine. Atwood's gutsy and unrelenting pursuit of abolition has already resulted in major legislative, political and judicial changes in the law, but most importantly, Atwood and his Texas Coalition to Abolish the Death Penalty, have had a significant impact on the most important court in America -- the court of public opinion."

>**Joan M. Cheever**, author of *Back From the Dead: One Woman's Search for the Men Who Walked Off America's Death Row* (Wiley, 2006)

"*Detour to Death Row* is an important source for teachers and students who want to know about the reality of the death penalty in Texas. David Atwood has detailed in numerous cases how Texas carries out its brutal system of state extermination. He has also included many documents from anti-death penalty organizations to demonstrate the horrific character of Texas's capital punishment system. This is a significant contribution from the founder of the Texas Coalition to Abolish the Death Penalty: Atwood shows how a campaign for human rights can be waged."

>**Roger C. Barnes**, Ph.D., Professor of Sociology, University of the Incarnate Word, San Antonio, Texas

Detour to Death Row
Table of Contents

Preface by Rosalyn Falcón Collier   ix

Introduction   xi

Chapter 1:   **My Journey**   1

Chapter 2:   **The Detour**   5

Chapter 3:   **The Faith Community**   11

Chapter 4:   **International Support**   17

Chapter 5:   **Sacred Lives**   23

Chapter 6:   **The Texas Death Machine**   29

Chapter 7:   **Unjust Laws**   49

Chapter 8:   **Other Sacred Lives**   55

Chapter 9:   **But what am I for?**   69

Chapter 10: **Final Words**   73

Appendix A: **Evangelium Vitae** (The Gospel of Life)   76

Appendix B: **Statement of the Catholic Bishops of Texas**   80

Appendix C: **Good Friday Appeal, U.S. Catholic Bishops**   83

Appendix D: **Dominican Sisters of Houston Statement**   86

Appendix E: **Sisters of Charity of the Incarnate Word Statement**   87

Appendix F: **Texas Conference of Churches Resolution**   88

Appendix G: **Baptist General Convention of Texas Statement**   90

Appendix H: **U.N. Report— Extrajudicial, Summary, Arbitrary Executions**   92

Appendix I: **European Parliament Letter to Gov. Bush**   97

Appendix J: **U.N. By-Country Vote on Death Penalty Moratorium**   99

Appendix K: **Capital Punishment,** Rabbi Samuel M. Stahl   100

Appendix L: **Homily,** Fr. Emmanuel Charles McCarthy   103

Appendix M: **Clemency Letter** from Bernatte Lastrapes   109

Appendix N: **Index of Case Law**   110

Appendix O: **Suggested Reading and Web sites**   113

Appendix P: **Clips From David Atwood's Archives**   115

Index of Names and Organizations   126

Acknowledgements: 131

Never doubt that
a small group of
thoughtful, committed
citizens can change the
world. Indeed, it's the
only thing that ever has.

Margaret Mead

Foreword

Eleven years ago—in 1997—Ann Helmke, the animating director of the San Antonio peaceCENTER, and I flew to Washington, D.C. to attend the first national conference of Organizing the Religious Community Against the Death Penalty.

Every time the state of Texas was mentioned, the audience hissed. They booed. We felt mocked and forsaken by hundreds of good, forgiving and godly people. We Texans lived in the death penalty capital of the world. We Texans executed more people in a year than most countries. We Texans were the enemy, the evil empire. We Texans were the killers. Boo. Hiss.

We slumped down into our chairs in shame, trying to be inconspicuous. Maybe we shouldn't have come.

On the last day of the conference we got brave – and maybe a little angry. Knees shaking and holding hands to draw strength from each other, Ann and I approached the microphone.

"You're not helping us," we told the assembled group. "There are good people in Texas who work hard every day to abolish the death penalty, who visit prisoners on death row, who comfort the families of the victims and the condemned, who write letters to the editor, who speak to faith groups and community organizations, who march on the street and meet with legislators. We don't need your ridicule and scorn: we get enough of that back home in Texas. We need your support."

Then we stepped off the edge of the cliff, not knowing whether we would crash at the bottom of the abyss, or if we would grow wings and fly.

"Why don't you have your next conference in Texas? Bring your insight, your energy, your forgiveness and your faith to the place where it is needed most."

We flew! Two years later, 300 religious death penalty activists met in San Antonio. Slowly, slowly Texans grasp that the death penalty does not work. Slowly, slowly the people of Texas sense the absurdity of killing people to show people that killing people is wrong. Slowly,

slowly the arc of the Texas universe bends towards justice – but it bends.

One of those good people in Texas who has worked tirelessly to abolish the death penalty— one of those people who have slowly, slowly bent the arc of the universe towards justice—is David Atwood. In more than 15 years of tireless activism he has done all of those things we recounted at the conference in Washington: written countless letters, delivered innumerable speeches, met with prisoners and witnessed their executions, testified before the legislature and wept with families. Countless times he has driven the 150-mile round trip to Huntsville to stand vigil on the eve of executions.

David has experienced ridicule and scorn. People have wished him dead. This perfectly respectable retired oil company engineer has been jailed for civil disobedience. Dorothy Day, the founder of the Catholic Worker Movement, once wrote, "An act of love, a voluntary taking on oneself of some of the pain of the world, increases the courage and love and hope of all."

In the life he has chosen (or, perhaps, that has chosen him) David has taken on some of the pain of the world. His faith-filled witness and prophetic voice have increased our courage, ignited our hope, and taught us the meaning of selfless love. The peaceCENTER is excited to publish this book—a combination of a memoir and a manifesto—and to share David's passion and faithful diligence with the world.

Rosalyn Falcón Collier, peaceCENTER
San Antonio, Texas, August, 2008

INTRODUCTION

When I moved to Texas with my family in 1971, I had no idea that I would end up visiting prisoners on death row, witnessing the execution of three people or spending five days in the county jail for committing an act of civil disobedience during an execution. Nor did I have any idea that I would devote more than ten years of my life working to abolish the death penalty in Texas, the most prolific state in the nation for executions. None of this was in my "life plan."

In 1971, executions were not being carried out in Texas, nor in any other state in the nation. However, they started up again in Texas in 1982 with the execution of Charlie Brooks by lethal injection, the first time this method of execution was used in the United States.

Since 1982, more than 400 executions have taken place in Texas. One hundred fifty two of those executions took place when George W. Bush was governor, and as of July 1, 2008, 166 have occurred under Gov. Rick Perry. No other state in the nation executes its citizens like Texas, a state that clearly has a love affair with the death penalty.

Most of the people who end up on death row in Texas are poor and cannot afford a good lawyer. A popular saying here is that "those without the *capital*, get the *punishment*." Texas has also sent a number of innocent people to death row over the years and, undoubtedly, several innocent people have been executed.

I first became interested in the death penalty while working as a volunteer on the Catholic Campaign for Human Development in Houston in the late 1980s. Later on, I was asked to visit some prisoners on Texas death row. These visits have helped me to understand that no one ends up there by mere chance. Most of the people on death row have had horrible childhoods; many have mental disabilities as well as drug and alcohol problems. Some are on Death Row because they were running in a gang. Many inmates become rehabilitated while on death row. The person that the state executes is rarely the same person who committed the terrible crime many years earlier.

After learning about capital punishment, I soon realized that there was no statewide, organized effort to fight the death penalty in Texas. Subsequently I worked to establish the Texas Coalition to Abolish the Death Penalty (TCADP). This organization started in Houston in 1995, but has since expanded to many other Texas cities. The primary work of the TCADP is to educate Texas citizens regarding the criminal justice system and the death penalty. We also promote legislation to improve the criminal justice system, try to save the lives of individual prisoners, work to improve death row conditions, assist the victims of crime and promote effective crime prevention measures in the state.

During the past 15 years, I have come to understand the historical, political and legal forces that perpetuate the death penalty in Texas. I have seen how the criminal justice system in the state is a flawed and biased structure that has resulted in innocent people being sent to death row. This system, from the original trial through the clemency process, is heavily influenced by politics and needs to be drastically renovated to ensure basic fairness.

I have worked closely with the faith community in Texas to promote abolition of the death penalty. At one time, the faith community was relatively silent on this issue. Thankfully, that is no longer the case.

My work to abolish the death penalty has also carried me into the international arena. I am convinced that international pressure is extremely important to abolishing the death penalty in the United States.

Anyone who works for abolition soon becomes aware of the pain of the victims of crime and their families. I try to be very sensitive to their grief as I work to abolish the death penalty. While I reject the argument that an execution brings closure or healing to the families of victims, I understand that the families have suffered grievously and are often re-victimized by the criminal justice system. I believe that the churches must do much more to bring healing to the victims of crime.

My work to abolish the death penalty has helped me to better understand the root causes of violent crime in our society. I have become convinced that the death penalty does nothing to address those root causes and, in fact, is a diversion. If our society truly wants to reduce violent crime, then we must do a much better job in addressing its source.

David Atwood standing in front of the Walls Unit of the Texas Department of Criminal Justice, where the death chamber is located in Huntsville. Photo: Houston Chronicle

CHAPTER 1
MY JOURNEY

I was born in Dover-Foxcroft, Maine, but grew up in Walton, a small town in upstate New York. I had a very normal upbringing – nothing unusual or spectacular. I went to Catholic Church with my mother and sister (my father was Episcopalian), played sports like other boys my age and did well in high school. I graduated from the University of Rochester in 1963 with a B.S. in chemical engineering and married Priscilla McKendrick who also graduated from the University of Rochester School of Nursing that year. After our marriage, Priscilla and I headed for New York City where I pursued an M.B.A. from New York University. Priscilla worked as a nurse to support the family while I went to school. While in New York (actually Brooklyn), our first son, Christopher, was born.

After graduating from NYU in 1965, I found employment as an engineer with Shell Chemical Company in Trenton, New Jersey. Before long Priscilla and I had two more children, Richard and Kathleen, both of whom were born in Trenton.

The 1960s were tumultuous times. President John F. Kennedy was assassinated in 1963. The Vietnam War was raging and both Bobby Kennedy and Dr. Martin Luther King, Jr. were assassinated in 1968. While these events greatly disturbed me, I believed that they were out of my control. I mostly concentrated on my family and my work.

In 1967, we rented a small house in Hopewell, New Jersey. We made many friends and living there was a wonderful experience. Priscilla was recruited into the local volunteer emergency squad. Soon, I also volunteered. The experience of doing this work opened me up to the suffering of other people.

While living in Hopewell, we often attended Catholic Mass at Princeton University. Songs of brotherhood, peace and justice abounded in the 1960s. Songs like Simon and Garfunkel's "Bridge Over Troubled Water" and James Taylor's "You've Got a Friend" were very meaningful to me.

In 1968, I was transferred to Shell's headquarters in New York City. A train from Philadelphia to the New York area went through Hopewell, so we decided to continue to live there although it was a very long commute. Those long hours on the train were an opportunity to read and think about how turbulent the world was and the need to create a more peaceful society.

My career seemed to be moving forward nicely. We enjoyed living in Hopewell, raising our family and doing our volunteer work with the emergency squad. In 1970, Shell decided to move its headquarters to Houston, Texas, which for me seemed to be at the other end of the earth. We moved to Texas in 1971 although it was very difficult to leave our good friends in Hopewell.

Transformation

Many unexpected things happened to us in Texas. Priscilla and I had three more children: Jennifer, Michael and Joseph. We were indeed a good Catholic family!

My work with Shell changed and I got involved in the area of occupational safety, health and environmental protection. This made my work more meaningful since it was people-oriented. I continued with this type of work for almost 20 years until I retired from Shell in 1991.

However, I felt like a fish out of water in the Southwest. I was not happy with my life despite the fact I had a wonderful family and interesting work with Shell. Something was missing. What was missing, I later found out, was a deeper purpose to life.

Eventually we became part of a small Christian community that operated a free health clinic for the poor in the Fourth Ward of Houston. One aspect of this community was having volunteers who worked at the clinic stay with us in our home. In 1974, we moved from our suburban home on a golf course in northwest Houston to the inner city to be part of this community.

Throughout this time, I sought to deepen my spiritual life through prayer. With my wife's support, I spent a month at a Benedictine monastery in Pecos, New Mexico. With time, I developed a better understanding of God's unconditional love for me and others. Jesus' teaching on compassion in the Gospel of Luke significantly influenced my thinking.

> *"Be compassionate as your Father is compassionate. Do not judge, and you will not be judged yourselves; do not condemn, and you will not be condemned yourselves; grant pardon, and you will be pardoned."*(Luke 6: 36-38)

I was also deeply affected by Jesus' teaching in the Gospel of Matthew that we should love our enemies.

> *"You have learned how it was said: You must love your neighbor and hate your enemy. But I say this to you: love your enemies and pray for those who persecute you; in this way you will be children of your Father in Heaven, for he causes his sun to rise on bad men as well as good, and his rain to fall on honest and dishonest men alike."*
> (Mt. 5: 43-48)

Eventually, I became very interested in peace, justice and human rights. I joined Pax Christi, the Catholic peace movement, and started to do volunteer work with the Catholic Campaign for Human Development (CCHD). During this time I delved into the teachings of Mahatma Gandhi, Dr. Martin Luther King, Jr., Mother Teresa, Dorothy Day, Thomas Merton and César Chávez, as well as many of the social justice documents of the Catholic Church.

Gandhi's teaching on active nonviolence had a profound influence on my thinking and it seemed to fit in well with what Jesus taught about compassion and love of enemies:

> *"Nonviolence (ahimsa) is the greatest and most active force in the world....nonviolence is infinitely superior to violence, forgiveness is more manly than punishment...If I am a follower of ahimsa, I must love my enemies..."*

Dr. Martin Luther King, Jr. also had a great impact on my thinking, particularly when he explained why violence was both impractical and immoral:

> *"Violence... is impractical because it is a descending spiral ending in destruction for all. The old law of an eye for an eye leaves everyone blind. Violence is immoral because it seeks ...to annihilate rather than to convert. Violence is immoral because it thrives on hatred rather than love. It destroys community and makes brotherhood impossible. It leaves society in a monologue rather than dialogue. Violence ends by defeating itself. It creates bitterness in the survivors and brutality in the destroyers."*

The lives and teachings of Jesus, Gandhi, King, Mother Teresa, Dorothy Day, Thomas Merton and César Chávez had a profound effect on me. I became a strong believer in the practice of nonviolence and much more sensitive to the sufferings of others and the need to reach out to those on the bottom rungs of society.

Death Row: drawing by Dominique Green

CHAPTER 2
THE DETOUR

      It wasn't until the late 1980s that I even became aware that Texas had a death penalty. In 1990, while I was serving on the Catholic Campaign for Human Development (CCHD), a Catholic nun, Sister Jean Amore, SSJ, asked our committee if we would financially sponsor a small newspaper named "The Endeavor" that was written by prisoners on Texas Death Row. Sister Jean was quite convincing and our committee agreed to help finance the newspaper.

I decided to research the position of the Catholic Church on the death penalty and discovered that the U.S. Catholic Bishops had issued a statement on capital punishment in 1980. The Bishops gave several reasons why they believed that the death penalty should be abolished:

> *"Abolition sends a message that we can break the cycle of violence, that we need not take life for life, that we can envisage more human and more hopeful and effective responses to the growth of violent crime."*

> *"Abolition of capital punishment is also a manifestation of our belief in the unique worth and dignity of each person from the moment of conception, a creature made in the image and likeness of God."*

> *"Abolition of the death penalty is further testimony to our conviction that God is indeed the Lord of Life."*

> *"Abolition of the death penalty is most consonant with the example of Jesus, who both taught and practiced the forgiveness of injustice and who came 'to give his life as a ransom for many' (Mark 10: 41)."*

I also began to research the status of the death penalty in Texas and the United States and was shocked to discover that the United States was the only western, industrialized nation that continued to execute its citizens. It had essentially been abolished by law or practice in Europe, Canada, Mexico and many other nations.

I found that the death penalty had been abolished in the U.S. in 1972, in a landmark case called *Furman v. Georgia*. The U.S. Supreme Court ruled that because the death penalty was being applied in an arbitrary and capricious manner, it was therefore unconstitutional. But four years later, after individual states amended their laws, the death penalty was upheld and states began making plans to resume executions.

The first inmate to be executed in Texas under the new law was Charlie Brooks. He was executed on Dec. 7, 1982 by lethal injection, the first time lethal injection had been used in the United States.

My research led me to another discovery: 38 states had the death penalty and 12 did not. Some states, such as Michigan, had not executed anyone in more than 150 years! Many of the states that had a death penalty statute had never or rarely executed anyone. Most executions took place in the South, with Texas leading the pack by a wide margin. Not only that, Harris County (Houston), where I lived, had more executions than any state in the nation, except for Texas!

I discovered that the death penalty in Texas was tainted with racism. African Americans were disproportionately represented on death row (40% vs. 12% in the general population). This was not a new development. In 1924, Texas abandoned the practice of scattered hangings throughout the state by installing a new electric chair in its prison in Huntsville. It inaugurated the new electric chair by executing five black men on February 8, 1924. The executions were supervised by a new warden because the old warden, Captain R.F. Coleman, resigned writing that, "a warden can't be a warden and a killer too."

I also discovered that there was no statewide movement to abolish the death penalty. Dr. Rick Halperin, a professor at Southern Methodist University and a member of Amnesty International in Dallas, had been working against the death penalty for a number of years and had organized a march against the death penalty in 1991. (Texans Against State Killing March) The 158-mile march started in Huntsville and ended up in Austin.

Also, there had also been several high profile campaigns to free certain death row prisoners believed to be innocent – Clarence Brandley, Gary Graham (aka Shaka Sankofa) and Ricardo Aldape Guerra. The SHAPE (Self-Help for African People through Education) Community Center in Houston had been deeply involved in these campaigns.

Compelled by this information, and encouraged by the National Coalition to Abolish the Death Penalty in Washington D.C., which was itself a fledgling organization at this time, a small group of activists in Houston began meeting in the mid 1990s. We called ourselves the Texas Coalition to Abolish the Death Penalty (TCADP). Soon, people in other parts of the state joined the group and eventually the TCADP became a statewide organization with chapters in Houston, Dallas, Ft. Worth, Austin, San Antonio, College Station, El Paso, Victoria, Beaumont, Corpus Christi, the Rio Grande Valley and Lubbock.

The primary mission of the TCADP was to educate the citizens of Texas about the realities of the death penalty. We believed that Texans would reject the death penalty once they were properly educated on the subject. We stressed the following points:

1. The death penalty is unnecessary for the protection of society. Society can be protected by long-term incarceration of offenders.

2. The death penalty does not deter violent crime by others.

3. The Texas criminal justice system is imperfect and innocent people have been sentenced to death.

4. A person who is poor normally does not get as good a legal defense as someone who has the financial resources to hire his own attorney.

5. There is systematic racism in the criminal justice system.

6. Juvenile offenders, people with severe mental disabilities and rehabilitated people are not excluded from the death penalty, but should be.

7. The death penalty does not bring closure or healing to the families of victims, but only creates another set of victims - the families and friends of the executed.

8. The death penalty is charged with politics.

9. The death penalty is very expensive to carry out. This is because of the lengthy legal proceedings involved in a capital case.

10. Money wasted on the death penalty could better be used on effective crime prevention programs such as improved youth and family services, drug and alcohol rehabilitation programs, mental health services and anti-gang programs.

Most of these "points" about the death penalty are as true today as they were in the mid 1990s. The only major changes that have taken place in the past 10 years are because of decisions handed down by the U.S. Supreme Court. In 2002, the Court ruled in *Atkins v. Virginia* that people with mental retardation are no longer eligible for the death penalty. In 2005, the Court ruled in *Roper v. Simmons* that "juvenile offenders" (those who were 17 at the time of the crime) were no longer eligible for the death penalty. Also, in June 2005, the Texas Legislature approved of life without parole (LWOP) as an optional punishment for capital murder.

When we spoke in a church, we would also emphasize the moral issue — life is sacred — thus the death penalty is a grave human rights abuse.

Our efforts to organize were soon rewarded. In 1997, the National Coalition to Abolish the Death Penalty (NCADP) held its annual conference in Houston. In 1998, *The Journey of Hope ...From Violence to Healing*, led by Bill Pelke, George White, Abe

Bonowitz and Sister Helen Prejean toured Texas and ended its tour with a large anti-death penalty rally at the State Capitol in Austin.

With my volunteer work for peace, social justice and human rights rapidly growing, my interest in working for Shell Oil began to diminish. In 1991, Shell decided to cut its corporate staff because of a sluggish economy. I and many other long-term employees were offered early retirement packages. I decided to accept the offer and subsequently went to work for a consulting firm in Houston. This work lasted several years. However, as time passed, I reduced my consulting work to devote more time to my volunteer work against the death penalty. Needless to say, this posed a significant financial sacrifice for my family.

I recognized early on that abolishing the death penalty in Texas was a Herculean task, particularly since we had minimal funds to carry out the work. We had to rely on the work of many volunteers, most of whom had regular jobs, to even begin to take on this challenge. It soon became obvious that, if we were going to accomplish anything, we had to enlist the faith community to help us. Naturally, I turned to the Catholic Church.

This painting by Jude Thetford of Mary holding Jesus after he was taken down from the cross was made into postcards which were distributed throughout the state.

CHAPTER 3
THE FAITH COMMUNITY

Although the U.S. Catholic Bishops had issued a statement against the death penalty in 1980, little had been said publicly about the subject in Texas following the publication of that document. In the mid 1990s I began to write letters to church officials and also to the editor of the Catholic newspaper in Houston, *The Texas Catholic Herald*. The responses to my letters in the *Herald* were usually letters from other Catholics who strongly supported the death penalty. I soon realized that Catholics in

Texas were not that much different from the general public when it came to this issue. The death penalty was part of the culture of Texas.

In 1995, Pope John Paul II wrote the encyclical *Evangelium Vitae* (The Gospel of Life) which spoke of the sanctity of human life. The encyclical included a section on capital punishment which said that the death penalty should not be used *"except when it would not be possible to otherwise defend society...Today, however, such cases are rare, if not practically non-existent."* (Appendix A)

Bishop Joseph A. Fiorenza of the Diocese of Galveston-Houston spoke out against the death penalty several times, saying that people who opposed abortion should also oppose the death penalty, and vice versa. Then, in 1997, the Catholic Bishops of Texas issued a strong statement against the death penalty in which they said that the State of Texas was *"usurping the sovereign dominion of God over human life by employing capital punishment for heinous crimes."* (Appendix B)

The U.S. Catholic Bishops and the Vatican also took stronger positions against the death penalty between 1995-2000. In 1997, the *Catholic Catechism* was revised to read:

> *"If ...non-lethal means are sufficient to defend and protect people's safety from the aggressor, authority will limit itself to such means, as these are more in keeping with the concrete conditions of the common good and more in conformity with the dignity of the human person. Today, in fact, as a consequence of the possibilities which the state has for effectively preventing crime by rendering one who has committed an offense incapable of doing harm - without definitively taking away from him the possibility of redeeming himself - the cases in which the execution of the offender is an absolute necessity are very rare, if not practically* non-existent."

Then, on Good Friday in 1999, the U.S. Catholic Bishops issued a statement against the death penalty:

> *"We see the death penalty as perpetuating a cycle of violence and promoting a sense of vengeance in our culture...we cannot teach that killing is wrong by killing.... we oppose capital punishment not just for what it does to those guilty of horrible crimes, but for what it does to all of us as a society...Increasing reliance on the death penalty diminishes us and is a sign of growing disrespect for human*

life...the death penalty offers the tragic illusion that that we can defend life by taking life." (Appendix C)

Finally, while visiting St. Louis, Missouri in 1999, Pope John Paul II spoke out against the death penalty, saying:

"The new evangelization calls for followers of Christ who are unconditionally pro-life: who will proclaim, celebrate and serve the Gospel of Life in every situation. A sign of hope is the increasing recognition that the dignity of human life must never be taken away, even in the case of someone who has done great evil. Modern society has the means of protecting itself without definitively denying the criminal the chance to reform. I renew the appeal......for a consensus to end the death penalty which is both cruel and unnecessary."

This was not the first time that the Pope had spoken out against the death penalty, but it was particularly significant since it occurred while he was in the United States. During this same visit, Pope John Paul II met with Missouri Governor Mel Carnahan and asked him to commute the death sentence of Darrel J. Mease, who had been scheduled to be executed during the Pope's visit. On Jan. 28, 1999, less than 24 hours after the Pope left Missouri, Gov. Carnahan commuted Mease's death sentence. The episode has come to be known as "The Miracle in Missouri."

Throughout this time, I received strong support for my abolition work from Bishop Fiorenza, the Dominican Sisters of Houston and the Sisters of Charity of the Incarnate Word. In 1997, the Dominican Sisters issued a statement against capital punishment saying,*"The Dominican Sisters of Houston call for the abolition of the death penalty in Texas and throughout the United States."* (Appendix D)

The Sisters of Charity of the Incarnate Word did the same in 2003 saying, *"We will work with others to call for an immediate moratorium on the death penalty and do all we can to bring about the abolition of the death penalty in our country."* (Appendix E) The Sisters of Charity also developed a wonderful publication on the death penalty called *Choosing Mercy*.

And, in 2005, the U.S. Catholic Bishops formally established a program called the Catholic Campaign to End the Death Penalty.

During this time, an artist friend of mine, Jude Thetford, painted a picture of Mary holding Jesus after he was taken down from the cross. We made postcards of the painting which were distributed throughout the state.

Also, I worked with Sister Elizabeth Riebschlaeger, CCVI, of Cuero, Texas, to commission a painting with artist Rafael Acosta which we titled "*Jesus, An Innocent Victim of the Death Penalty.*" We displayed this painting in several Catholic dioceses and also made posters from the painting which we distributed whenever we had the opportunity, such as the National Catholic Youth Conference in Houston in 2003. Sister Elizabeth and I also hand-delivered several framed posters to certain Texas legislators in the State Capitol.

The Catholic Church was not the only church speaking out against capital punishment. Many Protestant churches also had official statements against the death penalty. In 1998, the ecumenical Texas Conference of Churches issued a statement against the death penalty saying, *"We call upon all judicatories, churches, members and caring citizens to work in every way possible to oppose the death penalty and to work to create a humane, just and decent society...."* (Appendix F)

In 2003, the Christian Life Commission of the Baptist General Convention of Texas called for a moratorium on executions. This courageous step took place after the Southern Baptist Convention had issued a statement in 2000 supporting capital punishment. I was so happy that many Baptists believed that the death penalty was contrary to the teachings of Jesus. (Appendix G)

In 2008, the General Conference of the United Methodist Church meeting in Fort Worth, Texas, issued a resolution which called upon the Texas Legislature to either *"abolish the death penalty completely or to stop executions in the state until such time as all capital cases can be tried in a completely equitable way."*

The Quakers and the Unitarians in Texas would invite people to speak about the death penalty to their congregations and would regularly join us in speaking out against the death penalty.

Bishop Paul Blom of the Evangelical Lutheran Church in Houston, the Reverend Marilyn Meeker-Williams, a United Methodist minister in Houston, and Bishop Joe Wilson, a United Methodist bishop, would join our programs and speak out against the death penalty

When Governor George W. Bush, a United Methodist, was running for President in 2000, Bishop Wilson wrote him a letter in which he pleaded for a moratorium on executions:

> *"I continue to be dismayed by the number of execution being performed in the State of Texas...As a United Methodist, I hope you will seriously consider the stand of your church on*

the death penalty...My intent as an Episcopal leader of your church, is to appeal to your sense of fair justice and Christian conscience."

Despite this plea, Bush's support for the death penalty has never diminished. Similarly, U.S. Supreme Court Justices Antonin Scalia, Clarence Thomas, John Roberts and Samuel Alito do not appear to be persuaded by the pleas from the Catholic Church on this subject, although they are all Catholic.

It should also be pointed out that members of faith traditions other than Christian would also speak out against the death penalty. For example, when we held a press conference in Houston to protest the execution of Karla Faye Tucker in 1998, Rabbi Shaul Osadchey of Congregation Or Ami and Professor Selina Ahmed, a Muslim woman who taught at Texas Southern University, spoke at the conference. Buddhists have also joined our execution vigils.

Despite these public proclamations against capital punishment by church leaders in Texas, little has been said from the pulpits in individual Catholic and Protestant churches. This is undoubtedly because of the strong support for the death penalty among church members. It takes a lot of courage for pastors to speak prophetically to their flocks when they knew that many of their members strongly disagree with their message.

David Atwood with Vera Chirwa of Malawi, head of The African Commission of Human and People's Rights, November 28, 2005.

CHAPTER 4
INTERNATIONAL SUPPORT

During this time there was also significant international support for our anti-death penalty activities. A lot of this support was from people in Europe who came to Texas to visit prisoners on death row. The death penalty had been abolished in Europe and Europeans were shocked that the United States, which prided itself as being in the forefront of supporting human rights, continued to use the death penalty.

Canada and Mexico also expressed strong disagreement with the use of capital punishment in Texas. Canada publicly protested the death penalty when one of its citizens, Joseph Stanley Faulder, was scheduled for execution for the 1975 murder of Inez Phillips.

Former boxing champ and exonerated New Jersey prisoner, Rubin "Hurricane" Carter, and several other prominent Canadians came to Texas in 1998 to campaign for clemency for Faulder (see Appendix P). They were shocked by the callous attitude of Texas officials. In spite of protests by Carter and his delegation, the Canadian Government and U.S. Secretary of State Madeleine Albright, Faulder was executed on June 17, 1999. I and several others attended the execution vigils for Faulder in Huntsville as was the common practice of TCADP members.

Several Mexican citizens were on Texas death row and their government vigorously protested each time an execution was scheduled to take place. President Vincente Fox even cancelled a meeting with President George W. Bush to protest the execution of Javiar Medina on Aug. 14, 2002. When Mexico officially abolished its death penalty in 2005, the Texas Coalition gave President Fox an Appreciation Award at our annual conference in Austin. (A representative of the Mexican Government received the award for President Fox.)

In July 1997, following the execution of Irineo Tristan Montoya, a Mexican citizen who was convicted for the 1985 murder of John Kilheffer in Brownsville, I was asked to meet with representatives of the Mexican government in Houston to discuss violations of the Vienna Convention by Texas government officials. The Vienna Convention on Consular Relations, in effect since 1961, requires authorities to advise foreign nationals that they can contact their consulate for legal help if they are arrested. This requirement was not being followed by Texas officials.

Eventually, Mexico set up a program to alert its citizens living in the United States of their right to contact their consulate if they were arrested. The Mexican government also started to provide additional legal help for Mexican nationals on death row. Finally, Mexico sued the United States in the International Court of Justice (ICJ) for violations of the Vienna Convention. In 2004, the ICJ ruled that the sentences of 51 Mexican nationals on death rows in the United States had to be reviewed.

President George W. Bush asked the states to comply with the ICJ ruling. However, the State of Texas challenged the ICJ decision and Bush's statement of support in the U.S. Supreme Court. The Supreme Court ruled on March 25, 2008, in the case of José Ernesto Medellin, that U.S. states did not have to comply with the ICJ decision. Medellin was executed by Texas on August 5, 2008, despite objections from the ICJ and the U.N. Human Rights Office.

In the fall of 1997, I met with Bacre Waly Ndiaye, U.N. Special Rapporteur for Extrajudicial, Summary and Arbitrary Executions, when he visited Texas to study the application of the death penalty in the state. In 1998, Mr. Ndiaye issued a report which strongly criticized the death penalty in the United States.

Among other things, the report (Appendix H) stated:

- The execution of juvenile offenders and the mentally retarded violates international law.

- Lack of adequate counsel and legal representation for many capital defendants violates international fair trial standards.

- Race, ethnic origin and economic status appear to be key determinants as to who will and will not receive a sentence of death.

- The jury selection process may be tainted by racial factors and unfairness.

- Politics behind the death penalty raises doubt as to the objectivity of its imposition.

In 1997, Priscilla and I visited Italy at the invitation of the Italian Coalition to Abolish the Death Penalty. We met with several high-ranking Italian officials and participated in a major press conference in Rome to explain the situation in Texas. In 2000, the TCADP hosted the Italian Coalition during a speaking tour of Texas universities. (see Appendix P)

In 1998, the TCADP met with a delegation from the European Parliament that visited Texas. The delegation sent a letter on the European Parliament's position on the death penalty to Governor George W. Bush. (Appendix I) In 2000, the European Parliament adopted a resolution on the death penalty in the United States which:

- reiterated its call for the abolition of capital punishment and the immediate imposition of a moratorium in countries where capital punishment still exists;

- urged President Bill Clinton to grant clemency to Juan Garza (a federal prisoner scheduled for execution) and to impose an immediate moratorium on federal executions as a first step toward the universal abolition of the death penalty in the United States;

- called on all candidates running in the current (U.S.) presidential elections to endorse a moratorium on the death penalty and support the universal abolition of capital punishment.

In 1998, representatives of Hands Off Cain, an abolitionist organization in Italy, traveled to Texas to join in the protest of the execution of Karla Faye Tucker. Later, I was invited to participate in a conference on the death penalty that was organized by Hands Off Cain and held in conjunction with a meeting of the United Nations Human Rights Commission in Geneva, Switzerland. Sister Helen Prejean and attorney Thomas "Speedy" Rice of Gonzaga University School of Law also attended the conference as U.S. representatives.

Each year since 1997, the U.N. Human Rights Commission has passed a resolution calling on countries that have the death penalty to establish a moratorium on executions. On Dec. 18, 2007 the U.N. General Assembly, for the first time, passed a resolution calling for a worldwide moratorium on executions in a vote of 104 in favor and 54 against, with 29 abstentions. (Appendix J)

In 2001, I was invited by the family of Dennis Zelaya (aka Carlos Ayestas), on Texas death row for the murder of Santiaga Paneque, to visit Honduras, Dennis' native country. The Honduran Government had not taken a strong interest in Dennis' case and his family wanted it to provide more support. Dennis' sisters took me to meet with government officials and we held a major press conference in San Pedro Sula. Staying with Dennis' family in Honduras was a wonderful experience. Upon returning to the United States, I started visiting Dennis on death row and we have become good friends over the years.

Following the trip to Honduras, the Honduran government got more involved in the defense of its citizens on Texas death row. The Honduran Consul General in Houston, Lastenia Pineda, made a plea to Governor Rick Perry in 2004 to spare the lives of both Dennis Zelaya and Heliberto Chi, another Honduran on Texas death row, because the Honduran Consulate was not properly advised about the charges facing these men. However, Perry has refused to intervene. Heliberto Chi was executed on August 7, 2008.

A few years later, Priscilla and I had an opportunity to meet with Cardinal Oscar Andres Rodriguez Maradiaga of Honduras who was visiting Houston. We explained to the Cardinal that we were concerned that there were Honduran citizens on death row whose rights under the Vienna Convention had been violated by Texas authorities and enlisted his help in correcting these injustices.

In 2003, the Sant' Egidio Community invited me to participate in the **Cities for Life** Program in Rome, Italy. Sant' Egidio is a Catholic community which works against the death penalty worldwide. The community had been particularly active in trying to save the lives of Dominique Green and Johnny Paul Penry in Texas.

I asked Ross Byrd, whose father, James Byrd, Jr., had been brutally murdered in 1998 after he was dragged behind a pick-up truck in Jasper, Texas, to accompany me on the trip. Ross and his mother and sisters were all opposed to the death penalty despite what had happened to their family. They were a wonderful example of forgiveness.

Ross and I had an opportunity to speak to many groups in Italy and to also participate in the 4th World Summit of Nobel Peace Laureates in Rome. Mario Marazziti from the Sant' Egidio Community, Sergio D'Elia of Hands Off Cain, and U.S. attorneys Walter Long from Texas (a death penalty lawyer) and Adam Ortiz, a Soros Criminal Justice Fellow working for the American Bar Association National Juvenile Defender Center, also participated in the Summit which was hosted by former USSR Premier Mikhail Gorbachev. At the end of the Summit, this statement was issued:

> *"We the Nobel Peace Laureates gathered in Rome for the Fourth World Summit, declare:*
>
> *• Life can be defended only by life, never by giving death.*
>
> *• The death penalty humiliates those who are executed and the state which executes as well.*
>
> *• The world can give up the death penalty, just as it has rejected torture and slavery.*
>
> *This is why we join today with the world "Cities for Life - Cities Against the Death Penalty", promoted by the City of Rome and the Community of Sant' Egidio.*
>
> *We appeal to the governments of the world to stop all executions and to search for better instruments of justice, defense of human life and human dignity."*

Priscilla and I also participated in the **Cities for Life** program in Rome in 2005. As part of that program, the Sant' Egidio Community hosted a program called **Africa for Life**. Sant' Egidio invited the attorneys general from a number of African nations to come to Rome to encourage them to abolish the death penalty. During this time I had the opportunity to meet many of these men as well as Vera Chirwa with the African Commission on Human and People's Rights.

The TCADP joined the World Coalition to Abolish the Death Penalty and participated in the annual World Day Against the Death Penalty as well as the **Cities for Life** program established by the

Sant' Egidio Community. Sant' Egidio encourages cities around the world to light up a public monument or building on November 30 to show they are for life rather than the death penalty. In Texas, we decided to illuminate cathedrals in a number of cities since we knew that city officials would not agree to illuminate public buildings.

In 2003, 125 cities throughout the world participated in the **Cities for Life** program, including six Texas cities: Houston, Dallas, Ft. Worth, Austin, El Paso and Victoria. Beaumont participated in 2004 and San Antonio in 2005. In 2007, more than 700 cities around the world participated in the program. The number continues to grow.

In 2007, with the help of Sandrine Ageorges of France, the TCADP set up an international committee to achieve greater solidarity with our European allies and help fund our activities in Texas. With time, we hope that the committee will have representatives from all the countries in Europe that have expressed an interest in abolishing the death penalty. We believe that such international support will be needed to abolish the death penalty in Texas and the U.S.

The United States tries to ignore the fact that each year more and more nations around the world choose to abandon the death penalty. Currently, more than 130 countries have eliminated the death penalty either by law or practice. These international voices cannot be ignored. It is our fervent hope that, eventually, the United States will join the other nations that have abandoned this uncivilized practice.

Ron Carlson of Houston became close to Karla Faye Tucker when she was on death row for killing his sister Debbie. He is now a vocal opponent of the death penalty.

CHAPTER 5
SACRED LIVES

My detour to death row brought me in contact with many families of murder victims. These people have suffered grievously in ways that most of us can't even begin to understand. The families of murder victims have a wound which they will carry with them for the rest of their lives. Their anger is certainly understandable. When they tell me they want to see the murderer of their loved one executed, I don't argue with them. I just pray that, as time passes, they will somehow receive some healing and peace in their lives and their desire for an execution will diminish.

Some family members of murder victims have chosen a path other than seeking death for the person who murdered their loved one. They may not have started on this path initially, but ended up there after realizing that vengeance was a dead-end street.

One of the first people I met in that category was **Ronald Carlson** who lived in Houston and worked as a machinist. Ronald's sister, Deborah Thornton, as well as Jerry Lynn Dean, were brutally murdered by Karla Faye Tucker and Daniel Garrett in 1983. Karla was a wild young woman who had become hooked on drugs and prostitution early in her life. The murders took place after an evening of binging on drugs. According to Karla, the murders were not premeditated. Garrett, who was also sentenced to death, died in prison of liver disease in 1993.

Ron visited Karla on death row and saw that she had become a different person while in prison. He forgave her and didn't want to see her executed.

As Karla's execution date got closer, she wrote a letter to Governor George W. Bush and the Texas Board of Pardons and Paroles asking for clemency. In the letter she wrote:

> *"I am in no way attempting to minimize the brutality of my crime. It obviously was very, very horrible and I do take full responsibility for what happened...I also know that justice and the law demand my life for the two innocent lives I brutally murdered that night. If my execution is the only thing, the final act that can fulfill the demands for restitution for justice, then I accept that...I will pay the price for what I did in any way our law demands it...*

> *"It was...three months after I had been locked up, when a ministry came to the jail and I went to the services that night, accepting Jesus into my heart. When I did this, the full and overwhelming weight and reality of what I had done hit me...I began crying that night for the first time in many years, and to this day, tears are part of my life...*

> *"Fourteen years ago, I was part of the problem. Now I am part of the solution.*

> *"I have purposed to do right for the last 14 years, not because I am in prison, but because my God demands this of me. I know right from wrong and I must do right...*

> *"I don't really understand the guidelines for commutation of death sentences, but I can promise you this: If you commute my sentence to life, I will continue for the rest of my life on this earth to reach out to others to make a positive difference in their lives.*

> *"I see people in the prison where I am who are here for horrible crimes...I can reach out to these girls and try to help them change before they walk out of this place and hurt someone else.*

> *"I am seeking you to commute my sentence and allow me to pay society back by helping others. I can't bring back the lives I took. But I can, if I am allowed, help save lives. That is the only real restitution I can give."*

Despite Karla's plea, and the pleas of Ron Carlson and many people around the world, the Texas Parole Board and Governor George W. Bush would not spare Karla Faye Tucker's life. Ronald witnessed the execution of his sister's killer on Feb. 3, 1998, while hundreds of us protested outside the prison walls. (See Appendix P) After Karla's execution, Ron said:

> "The world is not a better place because the State of Texas executed Karla Faye Tucker. Even though Karla murdered my only sibling — my sister, Deborah, who had raised me after our mother died — I stood with her as one of her witnesses when she was executed. I was there to stand up for the Lord, for the strength of his love. Karla and I had both done a lot of wrong in our lives. We had both turned to drugs to heal our pain; we had both hurt a lot of people. But the love of Jesus Christ transformed us. We were able to forgive ourselves and each other. 'I love you, Ronnie', was one of the last things Karla said. I still carry that love with me."

Ronald Carlson still lives in the Houston area. He is still a strong advocate for abolishing the death penalty and I have come to know and admire him in my work against the death penalty. He is one of a growing cadre of people who choose to use their pain to make the world a better place to live for all of us.

Another such person is **Carol Byars**, who also lived in the Houston area and worked as a waitress. Carol's husband, James, was shot in 1977 during an altercation with his mother's next-door neighbor. He eventually died from his wound. The neighbor was sentenced to life in prison. Although devastated by the loss, Carol chose not to seek revenge but to become involved in our work to abolish the death penalty. She joined Murder Victims Families for Reconciliation and frequently participated in a speaking tour called The Journey of Hope...From Violence to Healing. Carol's life was truly a journey of hope. She once said:

> "We are told so many times that we are not supposed to forgive — that when people do horrible things to us we should do something just as bad in retribution. Those of us who know better — those of us who know the power of forgiveness - need to speak up...we need to challenge the mentality that compassion is a weakness. Compassion is the toughest thing of all, but it's the only thing that works to restore peace in our lives."

Carol believed so strongly that she participated in the 2005 Journey of Hope Texas tour while ill. Nine months later, on July 11,

2006, Carol died. I honor her commitment and passion to abolish the death penalty, as well as her memory.

Another amazing person I have come to know over the years in **Linda White**, whose daughter, Cathy, was raped and murdered by two boys in 1986. Because of their age, both boys, then 15 years old, were ineligible for the death penalty, but received sentences in excess of 50 years.

After Cathy's death, Linda returned to college and earned a Ph.D. in psychology. She also raised Cathy's daughter, Ami, who was five years old at the time of her mother's murder. After earning her degree, Linda taught a "death and dying" class at Sam Houston State University in Huntsville, home to Texas' death row.

After Ami grew up, she and Linda decided to visit one of the boys who had killed Cathy. The two women had both become proponents of "restorative justice" and wanted to take this step. After a lot of preparation, they visited Gary Brown in prison in 2001. The visit was soul-wrenching for both Linda and Ami, as well as for Gary, who was repentant for what he had done when he was 15 years old.

Despite their painful experience, both Linda and Ami would often speak out against the death penalty. Linda told of its negative impact on society, saying, *"I believe that the death penalty is about who we are as a society, not what the offender has done to deserve this punishment. As long as we model killing as an appropriate response, we will continue to be the most violent society within the highly developed nations."*

Ami would often speak about how the death penalty creates more victims. She said, *"When one loses a loved one to murder, that experience should increase our sensitivity to others, not dull it.....we must acknowledge that creating more victims does not serve justice or bring healing to anyone...."*

Another amazing person is **Jeanette Popp** from Azle, Texas. Jeanette's daughter, Nancy DePriest, was murdered in Austin, Texas, during the robbery of a Pizza Hut in 1988. Two men, Christopher Ochoa and Richard Danziger, were coerced by police into confessing to the crime. They were convicted and given life sentences. They spent 12 years in prison before being proven innocent and released after another man, Achim Josef Marino, confessed to the crime. Christopher Ochoa later went to law school and became an attorney. Richard Danziger became disabled after being severely beaten while in prison.

Jeanette was so upset about what had happened in her daughter's case that she became an advocate for abolition of the death penalty. She also ran for the Texas State Legislature in 2004 on an abolitionist platform, a very courageous move for someone in Texas. Jeanette often spoke out publicly against the death penalty saying, *"It is my wish that the death penalty be abolished in the State of Texas so that it can no longer be used as a threat to coerce confessions from the innocent."*

Ronald Carlson, Carol Byars, Linda White, Ami White and Jeanette Popp are five Texans who have had a great impact on my life. They are representative of thousands of other people in the United States who have lost a loved one to murder and yet choose life over death. There are many others, including Bill Pelke of Alaska, Renny Cushing of New Hampshire, Marietta Jaeger-Lane of Montana and Bud Welch of Oklahoma. Whenever I listen to any of these people speak out against the death penalty, I come to better understand the message of Jesus about forgiveness, compassion and mercy.

The Execution Chamber: drawing by Dominique Green

CHAPTER 6
THE TEXAS DEATH MACHINE

My detour to death row taught me a lot about the attitudes of Texans regarding crime and punishment as well as how the Texas criminal justice system works. The state has had more than 400 executions in the past 25 years, which is more than one third of the total number of executions in the United States. In some circles, the state has become known as the "Death Penalty Capital of the Western World."

Why are there so many executions in Texas? A former employee of the Texas Department of Criminal Justice once said that Texas was the "victims' rights state." But that is misleading. Polls have shown that Texans aren't that much different than other U.S. citizens when it comes to the death penalty. In fact, a 2008 poll conducted in Houston by Rice University Professor Stephen Klineberg showed that 55% of the people surveyed favored life without parole or a long prison sentence versus 38% who favored the death penalty for someone who had committed capital murder. Remember, Houston is in Harris County, which has more death sentences than any other county in the nation.

However, there is certainly a tradition of "frontier justice" in Texas that goes back many years. In the past, people were hung for stealing horses and other crimes less than murder. And Texas, like other states in the South, has a history of lynching African-Americans. This is described in the book *The Rope, the Chair and the Needle*: *Capital Punishment in Texas 1923-1990*, by James Marquart, Sheldon Ekland-Olson and Jonathan R. Sorensen (University of Texas Press, 1994) Today, some people describe executions as "legal lynchings."

Christian fundamentalism is also strong in Texas. Many fundamentalists believe that the death penalty is justified in the Bible. They often refer to texts in the Old Testament to support their position and downplay the teachings of Jesus on compassion, forgiveness and mercy. Dale Recinella's book, *The Biblical Truth about America's Death Penalty* (Northeastern, 2004) explores the biblical basis for the death penalty. Please note that many Jewish scholars dispute the suggestion that the Hebrew Scriptures promote the death penalty. (Appendix K)

Naked politics also plays a role in who lives and dies in Texas. Most politicians in Texas believe that they must support the death penalty in order to get elected. The governor and the state representatives and senators are, of course, all elected. The district attorneys are all elected. The criminal court judges, including those who serve on the highest criminal court in the state, the Texas Court of Criminal Appeals (TCCA), are all elected officials as well.

U.S. Supreme Court Justice John Paul Stevens once cautioned against judicial activism when he said: *"Present day capital judges [face] a political climate in which judges who covet higher office — or who merely wish to remain judges — must constantly profess their loyalty to the death penalty."* It is a fact that the only two moderate judges on the Texas Court of Criminal

Appeals in recent history, Charles Baird and Morris Overstreet, were voted out office.

The Texas Criminal Justice System

I have learned a lot about the Texas criminal justice system through my work on the death penalty. Before I got involved, I assumed that the criminal justice system was basically fair and treated everyone equally. The idea that politics, economics or race could determine the outcome of a trial was beyond my comprehension, as was the idea that an innocent person could end up on death row. However, I soon learned that I was dealing with a flawed system that was organized and operated to ensure that executions were carried out efficiently, regardless of whether justice was ultimately served

Texas law permits the death penalty to be used as a punishment for several types of capital crimes such as murder of a young child, murder of a police officer, murder of more than one person, and murder committed in conjunction with another felony, such as a robbery. If you have the death penalty on the books, you must have juries that can give that punishment for people found guilty of capital murder. Someone who has qualms about the death penalty will not be allowed to serve as a juror in a capital trial. This puts an immediate pro-death penalty bias into the criminal justice system.

Most district attorneys in Texas support the death penalty, a fact not surprising. However, what a lot of people don't realize is that criminal court judges are often former district attorneys. And when you look closely at the Texas Court of Criminal Appeals, you discover that most judges on that court very publicly support the death penalty.

Unlike many states, Texas does not have a statewide public defender system. A defendant charged with capital murder in Texas who cannot afford his own private attorney is provided with a court-appointed attorney who may be inexperienced, under-funded or uninterested in providing a high quality legal defense for his or her poor client. Often these attorneys are appointed by judges who want the attorneys to cooperate in moving their cases quickly through the system. Some of the appointed attorneys contribute to the judges' campaigns to get re-elected.

In 2001, U.S. Supreme Court Justice Ruth Bader Ginsburg noted in a lecture, *"I have yet to see a death case among the dozens coming to the Supreme Court on the eve-of-execution stay applications in which the defendant was well represented at trial. ."*

Although there was an effort to improve legal defense for indigents through The Texas Fair Defense Act of 2001, a well-staffed and well-funded public defender system still does not exist in many counties in the state. For example, in Harris County where many death sentences are handed out, judges still have the power to appoint attorneys for indigent defendants. Defendants without a lot of financial resources are still at a huge disadvantage in the courts when compared to someone who has the resources to hire his own high-quality legal defense team. It is a fact that just about everyone on Texas Death Row is poor.

Someone who is convicted of capital murder in Texas is able to appeal his conviction to the Texas Court of Criminal Appeals (TCCA). However, this court has a history of determining that egregious errors in the trial court (such as incompetent legal defense and the infamous sleeping lawyer) are merely "harmless errors." The TCCA has been accused of adopting the findings of prosecutors without question. Even Texas Attorney General John Cornyn, a conservative Republican who is now a U.S. Senator, once criticized the TCCA saying, *"A court is more that just a processor of cases on a conveyor belt. It appears that the [TCCA] is more concerned about the process than about justice."*

If the person convicted of capital murder and sentenced to death does not get relief from the Texas Court of Criminal Appeals, he or she may appeal his or her case to a Federal judge in the U.S. District Court, then to the 5th U.S. Circuit Court of Appeals and ultimately to the U.S. Supreme Court. However, the 5th U.S. Circuit Court of Appeals, like the TCCA, has traditionally been very supportive of the death penalty. The U.S. Supreme Court is also quite conservative and hears very few cases. Furthermore, in the mid-1990s, in an effort to speed up executions, laws were passed at both the state and federal levels to limit appeals. Thus, a person with some very good legal issues may have his or her arguments rejected in the federal courts or may not be able to even get into court to have the issues heard.

This, of course, brings up another point: the quality of legal defense during appeals. Attorneys who work on state appeals are appointed by the Texas Court of Criminal Appeals unless the prisoner is fortunate to be able to hire a private attorney or have one work for him pro-bono. Studies have shown that some attorneys appointed by this court are grossly incompetent and many are under-funded to do a proper job. This is particularly lethal because, if important legal issues are not raised in the state courts, they can be lost forever to the person convicted of murder and can never be appealed. If a defendant with legal issues that might exclude him from the death penalty receives poor legal assistance during his original trial and state appeals, he could very well be executed.

Racism in the System

Although the primary bias in the death penalty system is economic in nature, the system is also tainted with racism. Approximately 40% of the people on Texas death row are African-American versus about 12% in the general population.

Racism can enter into decisions by the district attorney as to when to seek the death penalty. Professors Jonathan Sorensen and James Marquart have concluded that, all other things being equal, a Texan who commits capital murder of a white person is five times more likely to be sentenced to death than a Texan who commits capital murder of an African-American. Furthermore, with the rarest exception, white people in Texas have not received death sentences for the capital murder of African-Americans. The 1998 murder of James Byrd Jr. in Jasper, Texas was one of those exceptions. Two of the three white men involved in Byrd's murder received the death penalty.

This isn't just a Texas issue. Amnesty International reports: *"Since 1977, the overwhelming majority of death row defendants [in the U.S.] have been executed for killing white victims, although African-Americans make up about half of all homicide victims. African-Americans account for one in three people executed since 1977."*

In 1994, U.S. Supreme Court Justice Harry Blackmun also warned of the role of racism in the death penalty: *"Even under the most sophisticated death penalty statutes, race continues to play a major role in determining who shall live and who shall die. Perhaps it should not be surprising that the biases and prejudices that infect society generally would influence the determination of who is sentenced to death...."*

Racial factors can also be involved in decisions regarding the jury selection. A study published in *The Dallas Morning News* in 1986 showed that African-Americans had a 1 in 12 chance of being selected to serve on a death penalty case, while Latinos had a 1 in 4 chance and whites had a 1 in 3 chance. In 2005, the U.S. Supreme Court ruled that **Thomas Miller-El**, who had been convicted of capital murder in Dallas in 1986, and who had spent 20 years on death row and faced at least 10 execution dates, either had to be released from prison or retried since it was obvious that race had entered into the selection of jurors during his trial. I believe that this has happened many times in Texas. Miller-El's case is the one that finally got the attention of the U.S. Supreme Court.

On March 18, 2008, Miller-El's attorneys worked out a plea deal in which the death penalty would be taken off the table, but he would have to spend the rest of his life behind bars.

With the spotlight on race provided by the Miller-El case, the problem of racism in the selection of jurors will hopefully be diminished in Texas and in other states.

Racism is the reason **Clarence Brandley** spent nine years on death row. He was almost executed before being found innocent and released from prison in 1990.

In 1980, a young white girl named Cheryl Ferguson was murdered at Conroe High School. The police suspected that the crime was committed by a janitor at the school. A Texas Ranger, when interrogating Brandley and a white janitor at the school, said, "*One of you is going to hang for this*." Then he turned to Brandley and said, "*Since you're the nigger, you're elected*." Brandley had an all-white jury at his trial and was railroaded to death row.

When it later became evident that Brandley had not committed the crime, Conroe authorities never admitted that they had made a mistake. They also did not pursue the two white janitors, when suspicions arose that they were the men responsible for the crime.

Brandley's story is told in Nick Davies' book, *White Lies: Rape, Murder and Justice Texas Style* (Pantheon, 1991), and the 2002 movie, *Whitewash*.

Racism was also clearly a factor in the case of **Napoleon Beazley**, a 17-year old from Grapeland, Texas, who, with two other young men, was involved in a 1994 robbery in Tyler, Texas. During the robbery, Napoleon shot and killed John E. Luttig, the father of a federal judge. At the time of the crime, Napoleon was president of his senior high school class and involved in sports. He did not have a criminal record and planned to go to college after graduating from high school. It was a tragic mistake on the part of Napoleon.

Napoleon's trial was clearly tainted with racism. He, too, was tried by an all-white jury. At the end of his trial, in which Napoleon was given the death penalty, one of the jurors stated publicly, "*The nigger got what he deserved*."

Napoleon had an excellent appeals lawyer — Walter Long from Austin. At Walter's invitation, Priscilla and I and some other anti-death penalty activists from Houston went to Napoleon's hometown to participate in a prayer service for Napoleon. I also went to the church in Houston where Napoleon's sister worked and had them sign petitions to the Texas Board of Pardons and Paroles asking that they grant clemency to Napoleon. (See petition cards in Appendix P)

Napoleon's mother and father, Rena and Ireland Beazley, both wonderful people, spoke out strongly for his life. They realized that he had committed a horrible crime, but knew that he was very young and did not receive justice during his trial.

Despite the best efforts of everyone involved — attorney Walter Long, the Beazley family and the activist community — Napoleon was executed on May 28, 2002. His last words were:

> *"The act I committed to put me here was not just heinous, it was senseless. But the person who committed that act is no longer here — I am...Tonight we tell the world that there are no second chances in the eyes of justice...Tonight we tell our children that in some instances, in some cases, killing is right...there are a lot of men like me on death row — good men — who fell into the same misguided emotions, but may not have recovered as I have. Give those men a chance to do what is right. Give them a chance to undo their wrongs. A lot of them want to fix the mess they started, but don't know how. The problem is not that people aren't willing to help them find out, but the system is telling them it won't matter anyway. No one wins tonight. No one gets closure. No one walks away victorious."*

Napoleon was a young man who made a fatal mistake that caused a lot of pain for many people. However, he was repentant for what he had done and wanted to make amends. He should never have been executed. In 2005, the U.S. Supreme Court decided in *Roper v. Simmons* to abolish the death penalty for juvenile offenders, but its decision came three years too late for Napoleon.

Racism can be found everywhere, and I found much of it in Tyler, Texas. I traveled there in November 2000 to hold a press conference to protest the execution of **Stacey Lawton** and **Tony Chambers**, two African-American men who were scheduled for execution that month. When I returned to Houston that evening, there was a threatening message on the answering machine in our office warning me to never go back to Tyler. The caller said, *"Don't you ever come back to Tyler. We'll take care of our Blacks up here."*

Despite our best efforts, Stacy Lawton was executed on November 14, 2000, and Tony Chambers on the next day. Ida

Cheatham, Tony's mother, stood with us outside the Walls Unit when her son was executed. She vowed to fight the death penalty in Texas forever. In 2007, she invited Priscilla and me to come to Tyler, Texas, to speak out publicly against the death penalty. We were happy to do so. Ida is a very brave woman.

On May 1, 2008, the results of a study on racism and the death penalty by Professor Scott Phillips of the University of Denver were published in *The Houston Chronicle*. The study concluded that African-Americans in Harris County, Texas, were more likely to get the death penalty than white people by a factor of 17-12.

It is very clear that African-Americans are treated more harshly by the criminal justice system when they are accused of crimes and their lives are seen as less valuable when they are victims of violent crimes. Is this not a classic definition of racism?

No Exclusion of the Mentally Ill

Although the execution of people with mental retardation was prohibited by the U.S. Supreme Court in the 2002 *Atkins* decision, there is no such prohibition for people who are severely mentally ill. At least 20 people with documented diagnoses of paranoid schizophrenia, bipolar disorder and other severe mental illnesses have been executed by the state of Texas in the past 25 years. (*Mental Illness and the Death Penalty Resource Guide* by Kristin Houle, September, 2007.)

Three people with whom I am quite familiar with are Larry Robison, James Colburn and Kelsey Patterson.

Larry Robison was diagnosed as paranoid schizophrenic at the age of 21. I know his parents, Ken and Lois Robison, who were both teachers and are wonderful people. Lois told me that mental illness ran in her family. Ken and Lois tried in vain to get Larry proper treatment. His treatment was sporadic because he was not covered by their health insurance and did not have insurance of his own. Mental health professionals told the Robisons that Larry was not well and would get worse without treatment, but hospitals routinely discharged him after 30-day stays because he was "not violent" and they "needed the bed." They were told that if Larry became violent, he would get the long-term treatment that everyone agreed he needed. In 1982 Larry had a psychotic episode during which he killed five people. In spite of his well-documented mental illness, he was given the death penalty and was executed on Feb. 21, 2000. Many of us who worked with Lois and Ken to save Larry's life stood with them outside the Walls Unit in Huntsville on the day Larry was executed. I will never forget the pain of a mother and father whose son is being executed. (See picture in Appendix P)

Ken and Lois have often spoken out about the need to improve mental health services in Texas. They ask, *"How can a modern, civilized society choose to exterminate its ill citizens rather than treat them?"*

James Colburn was diagnosed as paranoid schizophrenic as a teenager. He was raped at age 16, used alcohol and drugs and tried to commit suicide several times. He was in and out of mental institutions and crisis centers many times and spent several years in prison for various crimes. The treatment of his mental illness was sporadic because he did not have health insurance. In 1994 James murdered Peggy Murphy and received the death penalty for the crime.

Colburn's appeals attorney, James Rytting, and Colburn's sister, Tina Morris, fought hard to save his life, but he was executed on March 26, 2003. A Swiss photographer, Fabian Biasio, photographed Tina during the days leading up to the execution and on the day of the execution itself. The photo exhibit, titled *Diary of an Execution*, portrayed Tina's suffering. (See page 48) In 2005, the TCADP and Amnesty International co-sponsored the photo exhibit at the ArtCar Museum in Houston and held a panel discussion to highlight the injustice of executing severely mentally ill people. In 2006, Amnesty International USA published a detailed report on this subject, *The United States of America: The Execution of Mentally Ill Offenders*.

Kelsey Patterson was diagnosed with paranoid schizophrenia in 1981 and spent much of the 1980s in and out of jails and mental hospitals. Finally, in 1992, Patterson killed Louis Oates and his secretary, Dorothy Kaye Harris, in Palestine, Texas. There was no apparent motive for the murders.

Kelsey was given the death penalty and an execution date of May 18, 2004, was set. In a highly unusual move, the Texas Board of Pardons and Paroles voted 5 to 1 to commute his sentence to life in prison. However, to the amazement of all involved, this vote was turned down by Governor Rick Perry and Kelsey was executed as scheduled.

Patterson's mental illness was reflected in his last statement as he lay on the gurney: *"Statement to what? I am not guilty of the charge of capital murder. Steal me and my family's money. My truth will always be my truth. There is no kin and no friend; no fear what you do to me. No kin to you undertaker. Murderer...Get my money. Give me my rights. Give me my rights. Give me my rights. Give me my life back."*

Andrea Pia Yates is a severely mentally ill woman who killed her five children on June 20, 2001 in Houston by drowning them in the bathtub. The entire nation was shocked by the crime. Harris County District Attorney, Chuck Rosenthal, decided to seek the death penalty for Andrea.

In an effort to support Andrea and educate the public on the reality of mental illness, the Andrea Pia Yates Support Coalition was formed in 2001. In conjunction with Murder Victims Families for Reconciliation (MVFR), we held vigils outside the courthouse where Andrea was being tried and sponsored a special program at the Rothko Chapel in Houston. No one in her family wanted Andrea to receive the death penalty or even life in prison. They believed that she should receive long-term treatment for her illness in a mental hospital.

Andrea did not receive the death penalty, but instead got a sentence of "life in prison." Later, her sentence was overturned because an expert for the prosecution had misled the jury. In the second trial she was found "not guilty by reason of insanity" and was sent to a mental hospital for treatment. This should have been the outcome of her first trial.

A high profile case that is in the courts as this book goes to press is that of **Scott Panetti**. Scott was sent to death row for the murder of his mother-in-law and father-in-law in 1992. He has a long history of mental illnesss and was hospitalized 14 times between 1981 and 1992 for symptoms of schizophrenia, manic depression, auditory hallucinations and paranoid delusions.

A jury decided that Scott was competent to stand trial in spite of his obvious mental illness. He defended himself at trial dressed in a cowboy outfit. During the trial he wanted to call Jesus Christ and John F. Kennedy as his witnesses. No one can deny that his trial was a judicial farce.

In 2007, the U.S. Supreme Court blocked Scott's execution and sent his case back to a federal district judge to determine if he was "competent to be executed." To be "competent to be executed," one has to understand the connection between the crime and the punishment. In 2008, U.S. District Judge Sam Sparks ruled that Panetti was "competent to be executed." The case is again being appealed to the U.S. Supreme Court. It is obvious that Scott Panetti is a seriously mentally ill man. In the opinion of many mental health experts, a person who is seriously mentally ill is not as culpable as one who is not ill and, therefore, should be ineligible for the death penalty.

The State of Texas has spent millions of dollars on expensive death penalty trials for mentally ill defendants while its mental health system remains chronically under-funded. Texas ranks 47th in terms of *per capita* spending on mental health care according to the National Alliance on Mental Illness - NAMI. Many people with serious mental illness still languish on death row, waiting to be found "competent to be executed."

District Attorneys

District attorneys are elected officials who have a lot of power. If a case qualifies for capital murder in Texas, the DA has the authority to decide whether he or she will pursue the death penalty or the optional punishment of "life without parole." ("Life without parole" was passed by the Texas Legislature in 2005 and replaced a "life sentence" whereby a person could be eligible for parole after serving 40 years.)

One district attorney might seek death for a certain capital crime, while another might seek a lesser sentence for a variety of reasons such as:

1. The DA does not think that the crime qualifies as being the "worst of the worst."

2. The defendant does not have a criminal record.

3. The DA does not think that he has a strong case.

4. The defendant has a very good defense attorney.

5. The victim of the crime is perceived to be unimportant in the community.

6. The family of the victim does not want the death penalty sought for the defendant.

7. The DA does not want to drain the county coffers to prosecute the case.

8. The DA sees no need to seek the death penalty when society will be protected by long-term incarceration of the defendant.

All these factors mean that the death penalty is applied unevenly among counties within the same state. In places such as Harris County, where Houston is located, the district attorney often chooses to pursue the death penalty. Thus, about ¼ of all people on Texas death row are from Harris County. To put this into perspective, there are 254 counties in Texas.

The Harris County District Attorney's office is well-funded and staffed. Because it has tried so many death penalty cases, it has become very proficient at doing so. When you stack the DA's office up against a court-appointed attorney who may be inexperienced, uninterested and/or under-funded, it is easy to predict the outcome.

Unfortunately, some district attorneys resort to unethical practices to get a conviction.

Randall Dale Adams was in prison for more than 12 years and almost executed before being exonerated and released in 1989. When the Texas Court of Criminal Appeals finally overturned Adams' conviction after the U.S. Supreme Court intervened, it said: *"The State was guilty of suppressing evidence favorable to the accused, deceiving the trial court during the applicant's trial, and knowingly used perjured testimony."* Randall's story is told in Errol Morris' 1988 film, *The Thin Blue Line*, and Adams' own book, *Adams vs. Texas* (St. Martin's Press, 1991)

Kerry Max Cook was in prison for 22 years before being released in 1997, at which time the court released a statement: *"Prosecutorial and police misconduct has tainted this entire matter from the outset."* Kerry's story is told in Jessica Blank and Eric Jensen's gripping 2002 Off Broadway play, *The Exonerated*, and Kerry's own book, *Chasing Justice: My Story of Freeing Myself After Two Decades on Death Row for a Crime I Didn't Commit* (William Morrow, 2007)

U.S. District Judge Kenneth M. Hoyt ruled on Nov. 15, 1994, that **Ricardo Aldape Guerra**, who been sentenced to death in 1982 for the murder of a Houston police officer, should be either retried or released from prison. Judge Hoyt stated that the actions of the police and prosecutors involved in the case were *"outrageous, intentional and done in bad faith."* He further stated that their misconduct was *"designed and calculated to obtain... another 'notch' in their guns."* The Harris County District Attorney, Johnny Holmes, decided to drop the charges against Guerra in 1997, rather than retry him.

When **Delma Banks Jr.** received a stay of execution from the U.S. Supreme Court in 2003, his attorney, George Kendall, of New York City, stated:

> *"The Delma Banks case was fraught with material and intentional state misconduct. The State first promised to disclose impeachment and exculpatory evidence bearing directly on questions of Mr. Banks' guilt, innocence and eligibility for the death penalty, then failed in its legal and ethical duty to disclose it. The State also allowed its key witnesses repeatedly to lie to the court and jury...This*

misconduct by the State was exacerbated by its racially discriminatory and patently unconstitutional jury selection practices. Mr. Banks, an African-American, accused of killing a white victim, was sentenced to death by an all-white jury."

In 2004 when the U.S. Supreme Court overturned Banks' death sentence, U.S. Supreme Court Justice Ruth Bader Ginsburg wrote, *"When police or prosecutors conceal significant exculpatory or impeaching material, it is ordinarily incumbent on the state to set the record straight..."*

District attorneys will often say they are just carrying out the law. However, it is also true that they are politicians. Some of them travel to the State Capitol during the legislative session to lobby and testify in order to maintain the *status quo* and impose tougher laws. For example, some district attorneys fought tooth and nail against a law that would give juries in Texas the option of "life without parole" (LWOP) for someone convicted of capital murder, even though polls showed that Texas citizens would like to have that option.

When asked why he didn't support LWOP, the Harris County D.A. said that it would eliminate all death sentences, cost taxpayers more than executions, result in prison overcrowding, confuse jurors and create a dangerous situation in prison (see letter to editor in Appendix P). However, this has not happened in other states that have life without parole. All states that have the death penalty, with the exception of New Mexico, have LWOP as an optional punishment for capital murder. On June 17, 2005, life without parole was finally passed by the Texas Legislature, over the objection of the Harris County district attorney.

Future Dangerousness and Mitigating Circumstances

In order for someone who has been found guilty of capital murder to receive the death penalty in Texas, the jury must decide that the person will be a "future danger to society" and that mitigating circumstances such as mental illness and/or child abuse are insufficient to avoid the death penalty. District attorneys in Texas hire experts to testify that a person who has been convicted of murder will be a "future danger to society." One of these "experts," Dr. James Grigson, became so notorious for that testimony that he was nicknamed "Dr. Death." Grigson would often testify in court that a defendant would be a future danger to society although he had not even examined the person or given him a cursory examination! He even predicted that people who were later shown to be innocent would be a future danger to society. Randall Dale Adams—who was exonerated and released in 1989—was one of them.

An independent study carried out by the Texas Defender Service in 2004 (*Deadly Speculation: Misleading Texas Capital Juries with False Predictions of Future Dangerousness*) found that experts predicting a defendant's future dangerousness were proved wrong in 95% of the 155 cases reviewed.

The concept of predicting "future dangerousness" was rejected by the American Psychiatric Association in 1983. Most people on death row have not been violent while in prison.

A Flawed Clemency Procedure

If someone has been given the death penalty in Texas, and his state and federal appeals have all failed, the only way his life can be spared is through the clemency procedure. Clemency is meant to correct errors that were not addressed earlier in the legal process. It is also an opportunity for the state to show mercy in particular cases.

In Texas, the clemency procedure as administered by the governor and the Texas Board of Pardons and Paroles usually fails to correct mistakes or show mercy. When George W. Bush was governor he said that he would stop an execution if he had concerns that someone might be innocent or had not received a fair trial. That is a good sound bite, but the reality is that the evaluation procedure used by Bush and his staff was very superficial, at best. Otherwise, Bush would have discovered that many prisoners had ineffective legal counsel and there were serious questions of guilt in a number of cases. One hundred fifty two people went to their death under Bush's watch. I am convinced that there were a number of innocent people among those 152.

Governor Rick Perry has carried on Bush's merciless legacy and has presided over 166 executions by midyear of 2008!

The governor cannot grant clemency in Texas unless he receives a recommendation to do so from the Texas Board of Pardons and Paroles: a board that he appoints. Unfortunately, the Board does not meet to consider cases and has no written criteria for the approval of clemency applications. Rehabilitation of a prisoner is never taken into account. This system has been severely criticized by legal experts.

U.S. District Judge Sam Sparks once commented, *"It is abundantly clear that the Texas clemency procedure is extremely poor and certainly minimal. A flip of the coin would be more merciful than these votes."*

It goes without saying that there is little mercy in the Texas system. Even people like Karla Faye Tucker, who was considered reformed by everyone who met her, was not granted clemency by Governor Bush.

Kelsey Patterson, a severely mentally ill man, was denied clemency by Governor Rick Perry in 2004 despite the fact that the Texas Board of Pardons and Paroles had voted for clemency.

Innocents on Death Row

In July, 2001, in a speech before the Minnesota Women Lawyers, U.S. Supreme Court Justice Sandra Day O'Connor expressed her fear of the possibility of executing those who are innocent: *"If statistics are any indication, the system may well be allowing some innocent defendants to be executed."*

If you consider the obvious bias in favor of the death penalty in the courts, ineffective legal assistance for the poor, racism in the system, prosecutorial misconduct, limits on appeals and the lack of a true clemency procedure, it easy to understand how innocent people could end up on death row and be executed.

Randall Dale Adams, Clarence Brandley, Ricardo Aldape Guerra and **Kerry Max Cook** were released after it became evident that they were innocent. **Ernest Willis** was also released, in Oct. 2004, after being convicted of capital murder in the arson death of two women in Iraan, a West Texas town. Willis spent 17 years on death row before an arson expert ruled that the fire was likely an accident. These men are the "lucky ones" in the sense that they were not put to death.

However, several men with strong claims of innocence have been executed.

One of the first people I came to know on death row was **Richard Jones**. I met Richard when friends from Ravenna, Italy, Arianna Ballotta and Biagio Santoro, asked me to maintain contact with him after they returned to Italy.

Richard was a soft-spoken man with a great sense of humor. He was not anything like what I would expect a death row prisoner to be based on what you see in the media. Richard was on death row after he was convicted of murdering Tammy Livingston in Fort Worth during a 1986 robbery. As time went on, I learned more and more about his case and came to the conclusion that he was not guilty of murder and confessed to avoid implicating his sister who, he claimed, told him that she and her boyfriend committed the crimes.

After Richard had been on death row for many years, the State of Texas set his execution date for Aug. 22, 2000. His friends from Europe, including Arianna and Biagio, Michela and Carlo from Naples and Wendy and Jakob from Switzerland, came to Texas to visit him during his last days. In the afternoon on the day of his execution, we all gathered in the Hospitality House in Huntsville where the family and friends of the person scheduled for execution often stay prior to the execution. The prisoner can call the Hospitality House from the death chamber holding cell late in the afternoon. When Richard called, he spoke primarily to Arianna and his other supporters, but then Arianna asked if I would like to talk to him.

Truthfully, I was scared to talk to Richard. I didn't know what I could say. We had all worked hard to save his life, but it looked like we had failed. He was now scheduled to die in the execution chamber at the Walls Unit in Huntsville at 6 p.m.

I somewhat reluctantly took the phone from Arianna and asked Richard how he was doing. He replied in a low, despondent voice that he was not doing too well, but that he really appreciated everything that had been done to save his life.

I told Richard that he was in our hearts and prayers. He thanked me and I handed the phone back to Arianna. I was devastated. I had never had a conversation with someone just before he was about to die. I couldn't imagine what Richard was feeling.

About two hours later, just before 6 p.m., I stood with Arianna and other protesters outside the Walls Unit. Arianna was distraught because she believed in Richard's innocence and thought that this day would never arrive. None of us thought he would really be executed. We were all distraught.

Biagio, Michela, Carlo, Wendy and Jakob witnessed the execution. Richard's last words before the lethal drugs took effect were, *"I want the victim's family to know that I didn't commit this crime. I didn't kill your loved one. Sharen Wilson, y'all convicted an innocent man and you know it. There are some lawyers hired that is gonna prove that, and I hope you can live with it. To my family and loved ones, I love you. Thank you for supporting me. Y'all stay strong. Warden, bring it on."*

Richard Jones was the first death row prisoner I met. He helped me realize that prisoners on death row were human beings, not the monsters often portrayed by the news media.

Odell Barnes Jr. received the death penalty for the 1989 murder of Helen Bass in Wichita Falls. I never met Odell, but I met his family and became familiar with his case. His appeals attorneys, Mike Charlton and Gary Taylor, had evidence that raised serious questions about Odell's guilt.

One piece of evidence was a blood stain on his clothing that matched the blood of the victim. As Odell's execution date got closer, his attorneys had the blood stain carefully analyzed and discovered that it contained a chemical used to preserve blood in a test tube. In other words, the blood could not have come directly from the victim during the course of the crime. A logical explanation was that it had been planted on his clothing. This discrepancy and other information that created strong doubts about Odell's guilt were presented to the courts, the Texas Board of Pardons and Paroles and the Governor, but to no avail.

Odell's case received considerable international attention, particularly in France. Jack Lang, Chairman of the French National Assembly's Foreign Affairs Committee, came to Texas to visit Odell and to hold a press conference to protest his execution. We worked with the French Consulate in Houston and participated in the press conference which was held in Huntsville. There was a lot of French press at the conference, but the Texas media was typically sparse. After all, this was just another execution in Texas.

After Odell's execution, Mr. Lang stated, *"The execution of Odell Barnes is an assassination...How can Governor Bush pretend to aspire to be the President of the United States after having perpetrated such a crime? What credit would he have to demand respect for human rights around the world when he was the instigator of such a barbaric act?"*

Well said, I thought. By this time I was convinced that human rights, and even innocence, were not Bush's concerns. Odell's case was one of the first times that I became fully convinced that innocent people were in danger of being executed in Texas.

Gary Graham, also known by his African name, Shaka Sankofa, was executed on June 22, 2000. Although Gary had been involved in some criminal activity, it appeared that he was innocent of the murder for which he had received the death penalty.

Gary's legal defense during his trial had been abysmal. He was convicted of the murder of Bobby Lambert, a drug dealer, during a robbery outside a Houston supermarket. The only evidence against him was the testimony of one eyewitness who was not that close to the crime scene. Although the motive of the crime was supposedly robbery, the police found a large amount of money on Lambert's body.

As Gary's execution date approached, two very credible eyewitnesses came forward to say that Gary was not the person who had committed the crime. Also, the gun in Gary's possession when he was arrested did not match the gun used in the murder. This information had not been presented to the jury during Gary's trial.

Although Gary had excellent appellate lawyers, Dick Burr and Mandy Welch, they were unable to get back into court to present this new evidence because of changes in the law. Also, the Harris County District Attorney and the pro-death penalty organization, Justice for All, strongly lobbied for Gary's execution.

As Gary's execution date approached, we held a prayer service on his behalf at a Catholic church in Houston where his defense committee had met in earlier days. Many of his supporters from Houston and around the USA attended the service.

On the day of execution, hundreds of people gathered outside the Walls Unit in Huntsville to protest the execution. Members of the Ku Klux Klan were also there to support the execution. I thought to myself, "The Harris County District Attorney, Justice for All and the Governor of Texas all have good company today – the Ku Klux Klan!"

Despite the credible evidence pointing to Gary's innocence, Texas proceeded to execute him anyway. In his last statement Gary said:

> "I would like to say that I did not kill Bobby Lambert, that I'm an innocent black man who is being murdered. This is a lynching that is happening in America tonight. There's overwhelming and compelling evidence of my defense that has never been heard in any court of America. What is happening here is an outrage for any civilized country to anybody, anywhere to look at. What is happening here is wrong."

In 2007, *The Houston Chronicle* reported on the case of **Ruben Cantu** who was executed in 1993 for the murder of Pedro Gomez during a 1984 robbery in San Antonio. An investigation by *The Chronicle* indicated that Cantu may have been innocent. An eyewitness to the crime who had identified Cantu as the murderer later recanted his statement, claiming that he had been intimated by the police. Subsequently, the trial judge and lead prosecutor acknowledged that Cantu's convictions seemed to have been built on lies and omissions.

Also in 2007, *The Chicago Tribune* reported on two Texas cases in which innocent people appear to have been executed.

Carlos De Luna was executed in 1989 for killing Wanda Jean Lopez in 1983 during a robbery in Corpus Christi. *The Tribune* investigation showed that there was no forensic evidence linking De Luna to the crime. An eyewitness who had testified against him later said that he was not sure that De Luna was the robber. Furthermore, the police failed to pursue an alternative suspect who looked like De Luna and who admitted to others that he had committed the crime. Minutes before De Luna was executed he said, *"I hold no grudge. I hate no one. I love my family. Tell everyone on death row to keep the faith and don't give up."*

Carlos DeLuna's case was featured in the 2008 documentary film '*At the Death House Door*' by filmmakers Steve James and Peter Gilbert. The film tells the story of Rev. Carroll Pickett, who was chaplain in the Huntsville death chamber when DeLuna was executed. Pickett was convinced that DeLuna was innocent.

The Chicago Tribune also reported on the case of **Cameron Todd Willingham** who was executed on Feb. 17, 2004, for setting a house on fire, killing three of his own children. *The Tribune* reported that the initial investigation of the fire was seriously flawed and used archaic techniques. An arson investigator who later reviewed the case stated, *"There is nothing to suggest to any reasonable arson investigator that this was an arson fire. It was just a fire."*

The Texas criminal justice system is severely compromised when it is discovered that innocent people have been sent to death row and executed. It raises many questions about how many other innocent people are on death row and how many other innocents have been executed.

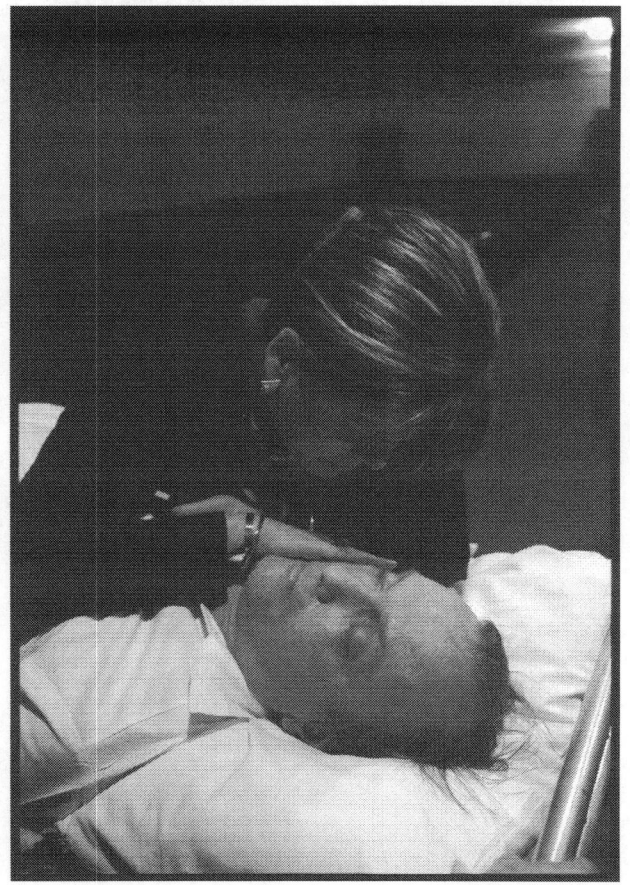

From top, left: snapshots of death row inmates. Tina Morris holding a picture of herself and her brother James Colburn. James was executed on March 26, 2003: Tina say goodbye to her brother, James, at the funeral home.

Photos © Fabian Biasio, part of the "Diary of an Execution" photo exhibit.

The entire exhibit is online at www.biasio.com. Follow the links to *Projekte & Todesstrafe*.

Protest March in Austin - photo, Austin American-Statesman

CHAPTER 7
UNJUST LAWS

As mentioned earlier, the TCADP started as a small group of activists in Houston. With time, however, we became a non-profit corporation, expanded throughout the state and ended up with 10 chapters by the year 2005. Most of our work was educational in nature — speaking in churches, schools, universities and else we were invited to speak. We participated in debates, wrote articles and letters to the editor, and spoke on radio and TV shows whenever possible. We held rallies and press conferences on high profile cases. We initiated public marches and protests against the death penalty. We held vigils in cities across Texas whenever executions took place. Many of us visited prisoners on death row and came to know their families. We believed that support of death row prisoners and their families, as well as the families of the victims of crime, were important components of our work.

In 1999 we also started to get active in the Texas legislative process. We established a separate group called *Citizens for Choice in Sentencing*. This organization emphasized improvements in the criminal justice system such a providing a life without parole option for juries. This option was finally passed into law (SB.60) in June 2005.

In 2001, a coalition of community groups came together to push for improved legal defense for the poor. The goal was to establish a well-funded public defender service as existed in some other states. What we ended up with was the Texas Fair Defense Act of 2001, which was an improvement over the existing legal system, but fell far short of a well-funded public defender system staffed with competent attorneys. The power to appoint attorneys was left in the hands of the criminal court judges whom we believed to have a prosecutorial bias. It was clear to me that some conservative judges and politicians did not want a public defender system since they knew it would be much more difficult to convict and obtain the death penalty for people charged with capital murder.

Also, in 2001, both houses of the Texas Legislature passed a bill to exclude the death penalty for people with mental retardation. This was a significant step forward. But Governor Rick Perry, bowing to the pressure from the district attorneys and victims rights groups, vetoed the bill. Despite this setback at the state level, the U.S. Supreme Court ruled in the *Atkins* decision in 2002 to exclude people with mental retardation from the death penalty. However, the Supreme Court did not tell the states how to implement its decision. Texas has never passed a law to implement the Supreme Court decision and cases of mental retardation are handled on a case-by-case basis to this day.

For years, Texas tried to execute **Johnny Paul Penry**, a man whose mental retardation had been well documented since childhood. (see Appendix P) Johnny was sentenced to death for the 1979 murder of Pamela Moseley Carpenter in Livingston, Texas. His death sentence was overturned three times by the U.S. Supreme Court because of problems with the instructions given to juries. On Feb. 15, 2008, the district attorney agreed not to seek the death penalty again when Penry agreed to serve three consecutive life sentences without the possibility of parole.

I visited Johnny on death row for many years and became acquainted with his sister, Belinda, who lives in Houston. Both Johnny and Belinda told me that, as a young child, Johnny experienced tremendous violence and abuse from his mother who was mentally ill. I suspect that Johnny would have turned out quite differently had he experienced love rather than abuse as a child.

Moratorium

The concept of a "moratorium" on executions became popular after Illinois Governor George Ryan declared such a moratorium in 2000. A moratorium is a temporary halt to executions while the death penalty system is studied. It is not abolition of the death penalty. In the 2001 Legislative Session in Austin, State Representative Harold Dutton from Houston introduced a moratorium bill. The bill was voted out of committee after a hearing in which former death row prisoners Randall Dale Adams and Kerry Max Cook testified, but the bill was not passed by the Texas House of Representatives.

To support the moratorium effort, the Texas Moratorium Network was organized and a moratorium campaign was launched throughout the state. Hundreds of people and organizations signed the moratorium petitions. Moratorium booths were set up at the Texas state Democratic Party conventions. Efforts were also made to have city councils pass moratorium resolutions. A few cities (and Travis County, where the state capital, Austin, is located) passed these resolutions, but with the pro-death penalty atmosphere in the state, we were unsuccessful in getting the large cities to pass moratorium resolutions. San Antonio and El Paso came the closest. However, several major newspapers in Texas did call for a moratorium on executions and one, *The Austin-American Statesman*, even called for abolition of the death penalty.

To support the moratorium effort, a video and study guide titled "Balancing the Scales" were created. Included in the video were exonerated death row prisoners Kerry Max Cook and Clarence Brandley, families of death row prisoners, a number of defense attorneys, a former judge on the Texas Court of Criminal Appeals and State Representative Harold Dutton. Thousands of copies of the video and study guide were made and distributed to people throughout the state, including educators and legislators.

Also to support the moratorium effort, I worked with Gary Bledsoe, president of the Texas branch of The National Association for the Advancement of Colored People (NAACP). When the NAACP held its national convention in Houston in 2002, it passed a resolution calling for a moratorium on executions across the U.S.

Also in 2003, The National Conference of Black Mayors met in Houston. I was invited to participate in a panel on the death penalty with Houston Mayor Lee Brown. The black mayors passed a resolution calling for a moratorium on executions during their conference.

In addition, the Catholic Church in Texas, particularly in Houston, made a strong push for a moratorium. Educational brochures were distributed in churches and petitions were signed and sent to Texas legislators.

In 2004, the Texas Democratic Party passed a resolution calling for a moratorium on executions, as well as other death penalty reforms in its party platform. This was a significant step forward because the Texas Democratic Party had been relatively silent on this issue up until that time.

Steps Towards Abolition

For most of us, a moratorium was a step towards abolition of the death penalty, our ultimate goal. However, it became obvious with time that the Texas legislators who supported the death penalty were not any more inclined to support a moratorium than they were to support abolition of the death penalty. They believed that a moratorium could lead to abolition and they wanted no part of it. Therefore, it became apparent that the TCADP should only focus on abolition, our prime objective.

In 2003, we joined with State Representative Harold Dutton and held a "Day of Innocence" at the Capitol in Austin. A bill to abolish the death penalty was introduced by Representative Dutton that year. This was the first time that the abolition issue had been raised in the Texas Legislature in a long time. Several members of the TCADP testified in favor of the abolition bill. However, the Republicans had taken over the Legislature and the bill did not make it out of committee. Abolition bills were also introduced in the 2005 and 2007 legislative sessions, but did not make it of committee. It seemed that our best hope for reducing executions rested with the U.S. Supreme Court. After all, it was this court, conservative as it was, that had excluded people with mental retardation (*Atkins* 2002) and juvenile offenders (*Roper* 2005) from the death penalty.

When the U.S. Supreme Court abolished the death penalty for juvenile offenders in 2005, 29 juveniles were removed from Texas death row. This was a reason for great joy, as many of us in Texas had been working for a long time to exclude juvenile offenders from the death penalty.

In 2007, we were pleasantly surprised when *The Dallas Morning News*, a conservative newspaper by all accounts, ran an editorial calling for abolition of the death penalty because it was imperfect and irreversible:

> *"This Board has lost confidence that the State of Texas can guarantee that every inmate it executes is truly guilty of murder. We do not believe that any legal system devised by inherently flawed human beings can determine with moral certainty the guilt of every defendant convicted of murder...If we are doomed to error in matters of life and death, it is far better to err on the side of caution. It is far better to err on the side of life. The state cannot impose death — an irreversible sentence — with absolute certainty in all cases. Therefore, the state should not impose it at all."*

As a follow-up to the Dallas editorial, I asked *The Houston Chronicle* to write a similar editorial. A number of years earlier, the *Chronicle* had stated in an editorial that if Texas did not fix its flawed death penalty system, it should stop executing people. Clearly, the flawed system had not been fixed. However, rather than running its own editorial calling for abolition, it printed an op-ed which I had submitted. It was not as influential as a *Chronicle* editorial, but was better than nothing.

At our annual conference in 2008, the TCADP awarded *The Dallas Morning News* with our Courage Award.

Our legislative efforts had some limited successes. However, major improvements such as a moratorium on executions or abolition of the death penalty will probably not happen until the political climate of the state changes, or until the U.S. Supreme Court rules the death penalty to be unconstitutional.

Photo ©Ken Light, 1994
Glen McGinnis on his twenty-first birthday
Texas Death Row

CHAPTER 8
OTHER SACRED LIVES

My detour to death row brought me in contact with many prisoners and their families. This contact is one of the main reasons why I strongly oppose the death penalty. While not discounting that the people on death row have caused great harm, I have come to know them as human beings. I have seen their humanity. I have learned about what happened to them as children and I have seen many of them change on death row. I know that there is much more to their lives than the brutal murders that caused them to end up on death row.

The Mentally Retarded Man

The first time I attended an execution vigil in Huntsville, Texas, was Jan. 17, 1995. When I arrived at the Walls Unit close to midnight for the vigil, I noticed a small group of people who had gathered away from the larger group of protesters. They were huddled together with their arms around each other and they were crying and praying. They were the friends and family of **Mario Marquez**, the man scheduled to be executed in just a short period of time for the 1984 murders of Rachel Gutierrez, his 18-year-old ex-wife and Rebecca Marquez, his 14-year-old niece, in San Antonio.

Mario was a mentally retarded man with an IQ in the 60s. He had been brutalized by his father as a child. He and his siblings had been abandoned by their parents when Mario was 12 years old. In describing Mario's mental condition, his attorney said, *"I was never able to discuss the specifics of his case with him, but instead we talked about his favorite animals, things he liked to draw and how he missed being able to see his brothers and sisters."*

Mario's last words were simple: *"Thank you for being my Lord Jesus and Savior and I am ready to come home. Amen."* It was the first day of George W. Bush's first term as governor.

After the execution, a prison official wearing a cowboy hat and boots came out of the prison and lit up a cigarette. I was wondering if he was calming his nerves or congratulating himself for a job well done. Maybe both.

I experienced evil in Huntsville that night. A human being had been strapped to a gurney and poison was pumped into his body. I asked myself, *"If this isn't premeditated, cold-blooded murder, what is?"* Human life had unnecessarily been snuffed out and another set of victims, Mario's family and friends, had been created. I knew I had to fight this evil.

The Wrong Man?

I will never forget the execution of **Anthony Westley** on May 13, 1997. Anthony was on death row for the 1984 murder of Chester Frank Hall during a robbery of a Houston bait-and-tackle shop. Two other men, John Dale Henry and Tyrone Dunbar, were involved in the crime. Dunbar was killed during the robbery. Henry received a long prison sentence.

About 15 minutes before the execution was to take place, we heard a loud wailing sound coming from down the road leading up to the prison. When we turned toward the sound, we saw a group of 15 to 20 people rushing up the road towards the prison. It was Anthony's family and friends. Many of them were crying and some of them were so distressed that they fell to the ground. When they got to the area outside the prison where we were having our vigil, a young girl with the family broke through the yellow tape barrier and ran crying towards the prison door. She was restrained by prison officials who brought her back to where we were standing.

After talking to Anthony's family, we found out that they believed that he would get a stay of execution because another man involved in the robbery, John Dale Henry, had admitted to the murder and the recorded admission had been provided to the authorities. Shortly before 6 p.m., the family realized that the execution would proceed as scheduled despite the recorded admission by Henry. When the family found that out, they came rushing over to the prison from the Hospitality House in Huntsville where they had been staying.

Anthony's last words before he was executed were, *"I want you to know that I did not kill anyone. I love you all."* We tried to comfort the Westley family but, understandably, they were overcome by grief. (See picture, Appendix P)

The Brain-Damaged Child

Joe Cannon was a juvenile who was on death row for the 1977 murder of Anne Walsh, a sister of Joe Carabin, a San Antonio attorney who had represented Joe in a burglary case. Anne let Joe live at her home so he could remain on probation and avoid jail.

In the days before his April 22, 1998 execution, Joe's mother and sister came to Houston to plead for his life. They spoke on a local radio station and we held a press conference at the juvenile detention facility in downtown Houston to highlight the fact that Joe was only 17 years old at the time of the crime, had received a debilitating head injury as a child and was never able to attend school. However, our pleas fell on deaf ears and the execution proceeded as scheduled.

Joe's execution did not go smoothly. The needle came out of his arm and he had to tell the prison officials about it. We found this out from a news reporter who had observed the execution.

Joe's last words were, *"I am sorry for what I did to your mom...I could never forgive what I had done. I am sorry for all of you. I love you all. Thank you for supporting me. I thank you for being kind to me when I was small. Thank you, God."*

When Joe's mother learned that the execution had taken place, she collapsed outside the prison walls. It was a devastating day for everyone involved.

The Dominican

Jonathan Nobles ended up on death row for the murders of Mitzi Johnson-Malley and Kelly Farquhar in 1986. Jonathan, an addict, was high on drugs and alcohol when he broke into the women's north Austin aparment and killed them. While in prison, he became very religious and eventually became a Third Order Dominican, a lay brother in the 500-year-old religious order.

However, his conversion did not save his life. Bishop Edmond Carmody, Father Stephen Walsh, Deacon Richard Lopez and singer/songwriter Steve Earle witnessed his execution on Oct. 7, 1998.

In his last words, Jonathan first said, *"I know that some of you won't believe me, but I am truly sorry for what I have done... I'm sorry, I'm so sorry...I wish I could bring her back to you."*

He then quoted 1 Corinthians 12 from the New Testament: *"If I speak in the tongues of men and of angels, but have not love, I am only a resounding gong or a clanging cymbal...Love is patient, love is kind ...Love never fails...And now these three remain: faith, hope and love. The greatest of these is love."*

Jonathan then said, *"Father, into thy hands I commend my spirit"* and began to sing, *"Silent night, holy night, all is calm, all is bright, round yon virgin mother and child...."*

He never finished the song. After the words "mother and child," Jonathan Nobles, OP, died from the chemical poisons coursing through his body.

The Juvenile Offender

Glen McGinnis murdered Leta Ann Wilkerson during a 1990 robbery of a drycleaning store in Conroe. Glen was 17 years old at the time of the crime, which qualified him as a "juvenile offender." I knew of Glen primarily through his good friend, Karl Rodenburg, from Germany, who considered Glen to be his "adopted son." Karl would regularly come to Texas to visit Glen on death row.

Glen grew up in Houston; his mother was a drug addict who was incarcerated for long periods of time. He lived with his stepfather who physically, sexually and psychologically abused him. Glen ran way from home at age 11 and lived in abandoned houses in Houston. Eventually, he got into a life of crime and killed Ms. Wilkerson.

Three weeks before his scheduled execution, Glen was interviewed by CNN correspondent Linda Pattillo who asked him whether he believed the death penalty was a deterrent to crime. He answered, *"I didn't know the death penalty existed when I was arrested…so what is it going to deter? You're living on the streets. You're living day to day. You are trying to breathe. The death penalty? You see it every day where I grew up."*

I stood outside the death chamber in Huntsville with Karl Rodenburg on Jan. 25, 2000, the day Glen was executed. My dear friend from Germany was devastated, but he never gave up his dedication to visiting prisoners on death row and fighting against the death penalty.

In addition to Glen McGinnis, Texas has executed many "juvenile offenders" including Joe Cannon, Gary Graham, Napoleon Beazley and Gerald Mitchell.

Two Sons

It was a hot summer day on August 9, 2000, as the families and friends of **Oliver Cruz** and **Brian Roberson** gathered outside the Walls Unit in Huntsville to stand vigil as the scheduled execution of the two men drew near. Oliver Cruz was on death row for the 1988 abduction, rape and murder of Kelly Elizabeth Donovan, a linguist stationed at Kelly Air Force base in San Antonio. Brian was on death row for the 1986 murders of James and Lillian Boots, an elderly couple who lived across the street from him in Dallas.

An entire busload of people came to Huntsville from San Antonio in support of the Cruz family.

The families were joined by Father Charles Emmanuel McCarthy and Bishop John Michael Botean, both of the Eastern Rite Catholic Church. At 2 p.m. they led a prayer vigil, *Litany of Christ the Prisoner*:

> "Christ, a person condemned by the people, have mercy on us.
> Christ, a person humiliated, have mercy on us.
> Christ, a person regarded as expendable, have mercy on us.
> Christ, a person executed, have mercy on us.
> Christ, proclaimer of liberty to the captives, remember us.
> Christ, model for living, remember us.
> Christ, model for dying, remember us.
> Christ, a person praying for the executioners, remember us.
> Christ, a person jailed, have mercy on us."

At 6 p.m. the executions began. Brian was the first to go, followed quickly by Oliver. How efficient was the Texas death machine! The pain of both families was evident. An African-American women comforted a Latino woman who had collapsed in tears —two women caught in a moment of extreme pain and horror— joined by their common humanity and grief.

Oliver's last statement before he was executed showed that he was repentant for what he had done: *"First of all, I want to apologize to the family of Kelly Elizabeth Donovan. I am sorry for what I did to her twelve years ago. I wish they could forgive me for what I did. I am sorry. I am sorry for hurting my family, for hurting my friends. Jesus forgive me. Take me home with you. I am ready. I love you all."*

Later that evening at St. Thomas Catholic Church in Huntsville, Father McCarthy gave a homily on the subject of God's mercy. (Appendix L) He explained that God is a God of mercy, not vengeance, who would never condone what went on in Huntsville that day. I thought to myself that it was a wonderful message, but I wondered how many people who call themselves Christian believe in a God of mercy.

I didn't personally know Oliver or Brian, but I did come to know Yolanda Cruz, the mother of Oliver, after the execution. She explained that Oliver was mentally retarded. She also told me how he had made her promise to fight the death penalty after he was executed in order to save the lives of other prisoners. Oliver also wanted to have someone videotape prisoners on death row and show the videotapes to at-risk kids in schools so they wouldn't make the same mistakes that he had made. I included Yolanda Cruz in the "Balancing the Scales" video that we used to promote a moratorium on executions in Texas. Each year she has a Catholic Mass for Oliver and holds a Christmas party for children in the community at a local church in San Antonio.

The Informant

I visited **Craig Ogan** on death row for many years. He was convicted of the 1989 murder of Houston Police Officer James Boswell.

Craig reportedly had a very high IQ, which I could see after visiting him many times. He also appeared to have some mental problems.

When I would visit Craig, he would talk non-stop until I would raise my hand to interject a comment. Then he would smile and ask me what I had to say. Once I spoke, Craig would start talking again non-stop.

Craig had been an informant for the Drug Enforcement Agency (DEA) in Houston. One cold January night in 1989, fearing that he was in danger from some drug dealers, Craig asked the police to rescue him from a restaurant and hide him in a motel. The

Houston Police Department took him to a motel on the south side of Houston near the Astrodome. However, the motel room was too cold, so Craig called his contact and asked to be moved. Later in the evening, Craig saw a Houston police car outside the motel and went out to talk to the officers.

Apparently, Craig startled Officer Boswell, who drew his gun as he emerged from the police car. Fearing for his own life, Craig pulled his own gun and shot Officer Boswell. He was sentenced to death for this act and was executed on Nov. 19, 2002.

To the end, Craig believed that he had acted in self defense. His last words reflected that belief: *"I am not guilty...I acted in self defense and reflex in the face of a police officer who was out of control. Officer Boswell was angry at the time I walked up...."*

Craig did not have many friends and his mother lived in St. Louis. Before he was executed, he had asked me to get his belongings from the prison after the execution and send them to his mother. I picked up several bags of his belongings that had been placed outside the entrance to the prison after the execution. It was a painful experience to sort through Craig's personal effects which included a number of language books (he knew several languages), all his legal papers, and all of the letters he had received over the years.

I think that Craig was probably paranoid and that was what got him in trouble. He never believed that he should have been sent to death row. Truthfully, neither did I.

The Runaway

I have visited Chuck Thompson on death row for several years and he is still there as of this writing. Chuck was sentenced to death for the 1988 murder of Darren Cain and Dennise Hayslip during an argument. There were questions whether Dennise was shot intentionally and whether she ultimately died as a result of medical malpractice. While on death row, Chuck became a Secular Franciscan through the influence of Father Stephen Walsh. Secular Franciscans strive to follow the example of St. Francis of Assisi

When I would visit him, the conversation often involved the Catholic Church. At Chuck's request, I tried to get Catholic Mass restored to death row, but was unsuccessful. Also, I tried several times to get Cardinal Daniel DiNardo from the Archdiocese of Galveston-Houston to visit Chuck, but it has not worked out as of this writing.

In 2005, Chuck was successful in getting a retrial for the punishment phase of his trial. He came to Harris County for the trial and was housed in the Harris County Jail where Priscilla and

I visited him. Unfortunately for Chuck, he was not successful in getting a reduced sentence. Following the trial, some friends of Chuck's from Germany and I went to talk to his attorney to determine what should/could be done now. That evening, Nov. 3, 2005, we were shocked to hear on the news that Chuck had escaped from the Harris County Jail and was still at large.

That evening, Priscilla and I had a dinner date with an attorney from New York. I told my son, Michael, to call me if anyone showed up at our house. I was expecting the federal marshals since they normally talk to anyone who has visited someone who has escaped.

Sure enough, as we were finishing our dinner, Michael called to say that the federal marshals were at our home and wanted to talk to me. When we got home, the marshals asked if I knew anything about Chuck's escape or his whereabouts. I replied that I was as shocked by the escape as everyone else. I also told the marshals that Chuck had become a Secular Franciscan while on death row and I did not think he was dangerous. I told them that I hoped that law enforcement officers would not kill Chuck if and when they found him. That was my main worry.

The federal marshals left and I didn't hear anymore about Chuck until I saw on the news that he had been captured without any violence on Nov. 6, 2005, in Shreveport, Louisiana. I was thankful that he had not been killed during the capture. He was brought back to Houston under heavy guard and eventually transported back to death row in Livingston where he resides today.

How Chuck escaped from the Harris County Jail is still unknown to most people. Roger Rodriguez has written a book, *The Grass Beneath His Feet,* about Chuck's case. Some secrets about his escape may be revealed in that (as of this writing) not-yet-published book. I am sure that it will be required reading for the staff at the Harris County Jail.

When I visited Chuck after he was back on death row, I jokingly asked how he was going to resolve being a Secular Franciscan with his escape attempt. He gave me a big smile. Somehow, I think he will work it out.

The Artist

James Allridge never claimed innocence, but he did claim rehabilitation. He was on death row for the February, 1985 murder of Brian Clenbennan during a robbery of a Circle-K convenience store in Forth Worth. He took responsibility for the crime and often expressed sorrow for what he had done.

James had an older brother, Ronald, who was executed

in 1995 for the March 1985 murder of Carla McMillen during the robbery of a What-A-Burger restaurant, also in Fort Worth. James told me that his brother had mental problems that drew him into a life of crime. It was Ronald's influence on James that resulted in his committing some robberies.

After visiting James on death row for many years, reading his letters and looking at his beautiful art, I became convinced that he had truly become rehabilitated while in prison.

He was clearly one of the most accomplished artists on death row. His wonderful drawings of flowers and animals were seen by people throughout the world. I saw them as a pathway to his soul. (see drawings in Appendix P)

One of the people who was very impressed by James and his artistic talent was actress Susan Sarandon with whom he had developed a writing relationship. When James was getting closer to his execution date, I wrote Susan and asked her if she would come to Texas for a fundraiser that would benefit James, the Texas Coalition to Abolish the Death Penalty and several criminal defense organizations. She agreed and asked Sister Helen Prejean, whom she portrayed in the movie "*Dead Man Walking*," to join her. Susan joked that we would have both the real nun (Sister Helen) and the fake nun (Susan) at our fundraiser. The fundraiser was a huge success. It was the first time we had done anything like this in Texas. We honored the Texas Defender Service and the Texas Innocence Network for their courageous work and auctioned off several of James' paintings at the fundraiser which was held at the Warwick Hotel in Houston.

When James received an execution date of Aug. 26, 2004, Susan wanted to visit him on death row. I picked her up at the airport and took her to the Polunsky Unit north of Houston where Texas death row is located. It was surreal to be there with Susan and James as they visited. This time Susan was not portraying another person (Sister Helen), but was doing the real thing herself.

James asked two of his brothers, Sister Helen Prejean, Bill Pelke, Christa Dold from Switzerland and me to witness his execution. I dreaded this moment because I had visited him on death row for many years and cared deeply for him. I knew that he was no longer the person who had committed a senseless crime many years before. But I knew I had to be there for him. When I saw him strapped to the gurney in the execution chamber, I broke down in tears. An accomplished artist and writer, a genuinely rehabilitated person and a wonderful human being was about to be murdered by the State of Texas.

James expressed both thanksgiving and remorse before

his death. His last words were: *"I want to thank my family and friends; my family for all loving me and giving me so much love. I am sorry; I really am. You, Brian's sister, thanks for your love – it meant a lot. Shane – I hope he finds peace. I am sorry I destroyed you all's life. Thank you for forgiving me. To the moon and back – I love you all."*

This is how James Allridge evolved over the years he was on death row. He loved people and people loved him.

Following the execution, Priscilla and I attended James' funeral in Fort Worth. His mother, father and three surviving brothers were there as were many friends of the family. We felt very close to the Allridge family who had now lost two sons to the Texas Killing Machine.

The Gang Member

Dominique Green was with a gang of four boys who robbed and killed a man named Andrew Lastrapes in a Houston convenience store parking lot robbery in October 1992. He was 18 at the time of the murder. Dominique was given the death penalty and two other African-American boys in the gang were given long prison sentences. The fourth boy, who was white, did not spend any time behind bars. I always found this discrepancy in sentencing to be very disturbing. It was also not clear that Dominique was the person who actually shot Mr. Lastrapes.

I visited Dominique on death row for many years and found out that his mother, Stephanie, had severely abused him when he was a young boy (I later found out that Stephanie had been severely abused herself when she was a child.) Eventually, she kicked Dominique and his younger brother, Marlon, out of the house. Dominique ended up living in a rented storage shed, selling drugs and getting into a life of crime.

While on death row, Dominique gained many friends in Italy who became his supporters (Barbara Bacci and members of the Sant' Egidio Community in Rome.) Everyone was impressed with how he had developed as a person and how he helped out other prisoners on death row. We were also impressed with his artwork which dramatically illustrated what it was like to be on death row

As Dominique's execution got closer, his appeals attorney, retired Judge Sheila Murphy from Chicago, asked me to contact the family of his victim, Mr. Lastrapes. When I finally did locate the family in Houston, I was pleasantly surprised to find out that Bernatte Lastrapes, Mr. Lastrapes' widow, and her two sons, Andre and Andrew, did not want to see Dominique executed. Instead, they forgave him and asked that he be given another chance at life.

We held a press conference on behalf of Dominique at the University of Houston. David Dow, head of the Texas Innocence Network, Sheila Murphy and Bishop Joseph Fiorenza of the Diocese of Galveston-Houston attended and spoke out for Dominique's life. Andre Lastrapes also spoke saying, *"Killing him (Dominique) ain't going to bring my daddy back."*

Bernatte also wrote a letter to Governor Rick Perry and the Texas Board of Pardons and Paroles asking them to spare Dominique's life. (Appendix M) In her letter she wrote, *"All of us have forgiven Dominique for what happened. We want to give him another chance at life. Everyone deserves another chance."*

Judge Murphy and New Yorker Tom Cahill, author of *How the Irish Saved Civilization*, were able to get Archbishop Desmond Tutu from South Africa to visit Dominique. Dominique had read Tutu's book, *No Future Without Forgiveness*, and wanted to meet him. After his visit, Archbishop Tutu described Dominique as a *"remarkable advertisement for God."* Archbishop Tutu also talked with Bernatte Lastrapes by phone because she was too ill to make the trip to Livingston.

A wonderful concert was held at the University of St. Thomas in Houston on behalf of Dominique and Mr. Lastrapes. Sheila Murphy, Andre Lastrapes and Bishop Fiorenza all spoke at the concert, which was organized by Marlon Chen, a professional musician and orchestra conductor, who lived in Houston.

On the day before the execution, I took Andre Lastrapes up to the prison to visit Dominique where they had a beautiful reconciliation. Following the visit, Andre said to the press, *"Texas is going to put a righteous person to die like an animal, putting him on a table, strapping him up, putting those needless in his arms, putting him to sleep. We're not dogs. We're human beings just like anybody else. He's a human being, just like me, just like you."*

On the day of Dominique's execution, Oct. 26, 2004, both Andre and Andrew Lastrapes visited him in prison. Dominique gave them his prayer beads and a book of African prayers by Archbishop Tutu. It was wonderful to see this exchange. It was "truth and reconciliation" in action. (See photo in Appendix M)

The courts refused to intervene in Dominique's case and, despite the appeals from the Lastrapes family and many other people, The Texas Board of Pardons and Paroles and Governor Perry declined to grant him clemency.

Subsequently, Judge Murphy, Andrew Lofthouse (who

worked with Judge Murphy), Lorna Kelly from New York City, Barbara Bacci from Rome and I witnessed his execution. This was a very painful experience for all of us. For me, it was really devastating because I had witnessed the execution of James Allridge just two months earlier and had been on a 21 day fast leading up to Dominque's execution. I was in bad shape, both physically and emotionally.

Dominique expressed appreciation to his friends in his last words: *"Thank you for your love and support....I have overcome a lot....I am not angry, but disappointed that I was denied justice.... But I am happy that I afforded you all as family and friends...You all have been there for me....Its a miracle...I love you...Thanks for allowing me to touch so many hearts...I never knew I could do it, but you made it possible...You are all my family...Please keep my memory alive."*

I thought that Dominique had also acknowledged my presence at the execution and said something like, "Dave, you have your instructions." These words were not recorded in the prison's official recording of Dominique's last words. However, I know what Dominique meant — I was to continue to work against the death penalty until it was abolished.

Andre and Andrew Lastrapes, Dominique's common law wife, Jessica Tanksley, and many other people stood vigil outside the prison when Dominique was executed. The Sant' Egidio Community around the world prayed for Dominique during his last moments.

We held a funeral for Dominique in Houston following the execution. All of Dominique's family were there — his mother, Stephanie, his father, Emmitt, and his two younger brothers, Marlon and Hollingsworth. Marlon and his wife and child had flown in from Alaska where he was stationed at a military base. Jessica, Andre, my wife Priscilla, Judge Sheila Murphy and Kathryn Gough from Chicago, and Barbara Bacci from Rome were all there. Father Marco Gnavi of the Sant' Egidio Community in Rome sent a message to be read.

Dominique asked that his remains go to Italy after his execution. In November 2005, Priscilla and I fulfilled his wish by taking his remains to the Sant' Egidio Community in Rome. The community has built a monument in his memory.

The Grandson

I visited **Anthony Fuentes** on death row only one time, but I had become very good friends with his grandfather, Guy Landrum, and Guy's wife, Ursula, who had attended meetings of the Texas Coalition to Abolish the Death Penalty after Anthony was sentenced to death for the 1994 murder of Robert Tate during a robbery in Houston. There were several problems with the legal proceedings during his trial.

The evening of Anthony's scheduled execution on Nov. 17, 2004, was cold and dark as we held a prayer vigil outside the prison. Guy, who had essentially raised Anthony as his own son, decided to witness the execution as did Anthony's sister, Rachel. Ursula, Tammy (Anthony's mother) and the rest of the family were with us at the prayer vigil. As the time of execution approached, Ursula wanted to move up closer to the yellow barrier tape that was stretched out in front of the prison. Protesters were not allowed to cross the barrier tape.

As my wife, Priscilla, and I stood on either side of Ursula, I noticed that she was shaking. Something in me said that I had to do something more than just stand there holding my STOP EXECUTIONS sign. So, I gave my sign to another protester, put my cell phone, wallet and keys in Priscilla's coat pocket and crossed the yellow barrier tape as a protest to the execution. I was promptly arrested and held outside the prison until the execution was over. I was eventually sentenced to five days in the Walker County Jail for my act of civil disobedience, a small price to pay for protesting the execution of Anthony Fuentes. That was the least I could do for Anthony, Guy, Ursula and the rest of their family.

Anthony's last words expressed the peace he had achieved in his life and his hope that others would achieve peace in theirs:

> *"Sorry that I have to put my family through this. All of you know I got my peace. And I hope you find peace. And to the family, the truth will come out and I hope you find peace. I got my peace. I hope everybody has their peace. I am tired. I am going to be in your heart. I love you all. To everyone else, the truth will be known. It didn't come out in time to save my life. It is wrong to put the families through this. When it comes out, I hope it stops this. It is wrong for the prosecutors to lie and make witnesses say what they need them to say. The truth has always been there. I just hope everybody has their peace. Today I get mine. I love you all."*

Mario Marquez, Joe Cannon, Jonathan Nobles, Glen McGinnis, Oliver Cruz, Brian Roberson, Craig Ogan, James Allridge, Dominique Green and Anthony Fuentes were human beings with families and friends who cared for them. Whether they were guilty or innocent, their lives were sacred. Whether they were rehabilitated or not, their lives were sacred. And because their lives were sacred, we had no right to kill them.

David Atwood at an execution vigil for Stanley Faulder
photo from *Le Droit*, Ottawa, Canada

Chapter 9
BUT WHAT AM I FOR?

My detour to death row has always had me working *against* something — against injustices in the criminal justice system, against inhumane conditions on death row and, of course, against the death penalty itself.

Over the years, some people have said to me, "Dave, we clearly know what you are against. But what are you *for*?" That is a legitimate question and it should be answered. This is my answer:

I am for life in all circumstances. I am for life even when it may seem that someone does not deserve to live. I choose not to differentiate between "innocent life" and "guilty life" as some people are prone to do. If I recall correctly, Jesus came to save sinners.

I am for fairness and equality in society and in our criminal justice system. We do not have equality in society now and this often leads to violence and criminal behavior. If we want to reduce crime, we must reduce inequalities.

In addition, we do not have equality in the criminal justice system. The logo engraved over the U.S. Supreme Court building, "Equal justice under the law" is an ideal, not a reality. The most glaring inequality in the criminal justice system at this time is economic in nature. People who are poor are at a huge disadvantage in the courts compared to the rich. However, racial disparities also exist in the criminal justice system.

I am for restorative justice versus retributive justice. Retributive justice primarily focuses on punishing the offender, whereas restorative justice focuses on restoring wholeness to the victim and his/her family, the offender and society. Restorative justice has the potential for creating a much better society for all people.

I am for healing. The families of murder victims have a tremendous need for healing in their lives. This healing does not come from an execution, the criminal justice system or from victims' groups that promote revenge. It comes from a caring community that promotes reconciliation.

I am for addressing the root causes of crime. If we truly want to be "tough on crime", we must strengthen programs that truly reduce crime such as family and child protective services, drug and alcohol rehabilitation programs, mental health services and programs to reduce gang activity.

I am for compassion. Compassion for someone who has lost a loved one to murder is easy; compassion for a person who has committed a terrible crime is difficult. But I believe that compassion can develop if one comes to know someone and to understand his or her background. Many prisoners on death row had horrific childhoods. Many of them suffer from mental disabilities. Some were involved in gang activities where they did horrible things that they probably wouldn't have done on their own. Compassion is possible when you get to know prisoners, their families and their life experiences.

I am for forgiveness. Forgiving a person who has seriously offended you is very difficult. However, I believe that forgiveness is possible if one develops some compassion. Forgiveness can also occur if one realizes that anger and a desire for revenge can be very destructive to one's personal health. Forgiveness can take a long time and, ultimately, comes as a gift from a loving, merciful God.

I am for mercy. I believe that God is a merciful God. He does not want the destruction of his people no matter what they have done. Jesus said, *"Happy the merciful, they shall have mercy shown them."* (Mt. 5:7). He also said, *"Do not condemn and you will not be condemned yourselves; grant pardon and you will be pardoned."* (Lk. 6:37-38)   I believe that we should show mercy even when it is difficult to do so. We can do this and still have a just and safe society. A wise person once said, "Justice without mercy is no justice at all."

I am for the "least of these."   Jesus said that whatever we do to the "least of these," we do unto Him. He was talking about people at the bottom rungs of society – the poor, the vulnerable, the stranger, the sick and those in prison. I am for helping out the "least" among us no matter where they are found.

I believe that the people on death row are not the "worst of the worst," but the "least of the least." Many of them have had childhoods filled with abuse, neglect and poverty. They now sit in tiny cells in prison awaiting the day that the state will take them to the execution chamber and put them to death.

Dominique Green — photo by Patrick Murphy-Racey

Chapter 10
FINAL WORDS

My detour to death row has lasted many years. I am proud of the work of the Texas Coalition to Abolish the Death Penalty. Polls have shown that more and more citizens prefer a long prison sentence rather than the death penalty for capital murder. The number of death sentences has dropped significantly. Several major Texas newspapers have come out for a moratorium on executions, and some have called for total abolition of the death penalty. I believe that some day in the not-to-distant-future, the death penalty will be abolished in Texas and throughout the United States. That will be a wonderful step forward for humanity!

This work has been difficult because I have become knowledgeable of many horrific crimes and the suffering of the victims and their families. As I have said earlier, we must do a much better job as a society in both preventing crime and supporting the victims of crime.

This work has taken a personal toll on me in the sense that I have experienced frustration again and again. There have been more than 300 executions in Texas since I started to work to abolish the death penalty. I have come to know and care for a number of the prisoners on death row. I have seen them change while in prison. I have also come to know many of their families. It is always difficult to attend an execution vigil. It becomes almost unbearable to be there again and again with the family of the person being executed and to experience their pain.

It is also excruciating to witness an execution — to see someone killed right before your eyes, particularly when you have spent hours visiting with the person over the years and have come to care for him and his family. It is the material for nightmares.

It has also been very difficult to work on this issue because the culture of Texas has generally been supportive of the death penalty. People have often told me that they strongly disagree with my work to abolish the death penalty. A man once said to me that he would like to execute me! This continual negative feedback gnaws at you, so I have been very thankful when people have expressed appreciation for this work.

Finally, this has been difficult work because the people I have been trying to save have often committed horrible crimes and caused people much pain and suffering. It has taken a strong belief in the sanctity of all human life to keep on going.

My work against the death penalty has also taken a toll on my family — my wife, Priscilla, and my six children. In many ways, they lost their husband and father when I was off visiting prisoners, attending execution vigils, protesting, and traveling on behalf of this cause. They have also suffered financially since all the work was done without remuneration. I cannot express in words how much I appreciate their patience, their support and especially their love.

It is my fervent hope and prayer that this work to abolish state-sanctioned killing, which I believe God called me to do, will inspire others to speak out for life, even when it is unpopular to do so. Until we embrace the sanctity of **all** human life, the violence will never end.

.

...No man is an island, entire of itself; every man is a piece of the continent, a part of the main. If a clod be washed away by the sea, Europe is the less, as well as if a promontory were, as well as if a manor of thy friend's or of thine own were. Any man's death diminishes me, because I am involved in mankind; and therefore never send to know for whom the bell tolls; it tolls for thee...   John Donne

Appendix A
extracted from:

Evangelium Vitae (The Gospel Of Life)

Address By The Supreme Pontiff Pope John Paul II
To all the bishops, priests, and deacons, men and women religious, lay faithful And all people of good will on the value and inviolability of human life. March 25, 1995

53. "Human life is sacred because from its beginning it involves 'the creative action of God', and it remains forever in a special relationship with the Creator, who is its sole end. God alone is the Lord of life from its beginning until its end: no one can, in any circumstance, claim for himself the right to destroy directly an innocent human being". With these words the Instruction Donum Vitae sets forth the central content of God's revelation on the sacredness and inviolability of human life.

Sacred Scripture in fact presents the precept "You shall not kill" as a divine commandment (Ex 20:13; Dt 5:17). As I have already emphasized, this commandment is found in the Decalogue, at the heart of the Covenant which the Lord makes with his chosen people; but it was already contained in the original covenant between God and humanity after the purifying punishment of the Flood, caused by the spread of sin and violence (cf. Gen 9:5-6).

God proclaims that he is absolute Lord of the life of man, who is formed in his image and likeness (cf. Gen 1:26-28). Human life is thus given a sacred and inviolable character, which reflects the inviolability of the Creator himself. Precisely for this reason God will severely judge every violation of the commandment "You shall not kill", the commandment which is at the basis of all life together in society. He is the "*goel*", the defender of the innocent (cf. Gen 4:9-15; Is 41:14; Jer 50:34; Ps 19:14). God thus shows that he does not delight in the death of the living (cf. Wis 1:13). Only Satan can delight therein: for through his envy death entered the world (cf. Wis 2:24). He who is "a murderer from the beginning", is also "a liar and the father of lies" (Jn 8:44). By deceiving man he leads him to projects of sin and death, making them appear as goals and fruits of life.

54. As explicitly formulated, the precept "You shall not kill" is strongly negative: it indicates the extreme limit which can never be exceeded. Implicitly, however, it encourages a positive attitude of absolute respect for life; it leads to the promotion of life and to progress along the way of a love which gives, receives and serves. The people of the Covenant, although slowly and with some contradictions, progressively matured in this way of thinking, and thus

prepared for the great proclamation of Jesus that the commandment to love one's neighbour is like the commandment to love God; "on these two commandments depend all the law and the prophets" (cf. Mt 22:36-40). Saint Paul emphasizes that "the commandment ... you shall not kill ... and any other commandment, are summed up in this phrase: 'You shall love your neighbour as yourself'" (Rom 13:9; cf. Gal 5:14). Taken up and brought to fulfilment in the New Law, the commandment "You shall not kill" stands as an indispensable condition for being able "to enter life" (cf. Mt 19:16-19). In this same perspective, the words of the Apostle John have a categorical ring: "Anyone who hates his brother is a murderer, and you know that no murderer has eternal life abiding in him" (1 Jn 3:15).

From the beginning, the living Tradition of the Church—as shown by the Didache, the most ancient non-biblical Christian writing—categorically repeated the commandment "You shall not kill": "There are two ways, a way of life and a way of death; there is a great difference between them... In accordance with the precept of the teaching: you shall not kill... you shall not put a child to death by abortion nor kill it once it is born ... The way of death is this: ... they show no compassion for the poor, they do not suffer with the suffering, they do not acknowledge their Creator, they kill their children and by abortion cause God's creatures to perish; they drive away the needy, oppress the suffering, they are advocates of the rich and unjust judges of the poor; they are filled with every sin. May you be able to stay ever apart, O children, from all these sins!".

As time passed, the Church's Tradition has always consistently taught the absolute and unchanging value of the commandment "You shall not kill". It is a known fact that in the first centuries, murder was put among the three most serious sins—along with apostasy and adultery—and required a particularly heavy and lengthy public penance before the repentant murderer could be granted forgiveness and readmission to the ecclesial community.

55. This should not cause surprise: to kill a human being, in whom the image of God is present, is a particularly serious sin. Only God is the master of life! Yet from the beginning, faced with the many and often tragic cases which occur in the life of individuals and society, Christian reflection has sought a fuller and deeper understanding of what God's commandment prohibits and prescribes. There are in fact situations in which values proposed by God's Law seem to involve a genuine paradox. This happens for example in the case of legitimate defence, in which the right to protect one's own life and the duty not to harm someone else's life are difficult to reconcile in practice. Certainly, the intrinsic value of life and the

duty to love oneself no less than others are the basis of a true right to self-defence. The demanding commandment of love of neighbour, set forth in the Old Testament and confirmed by Jesus, itself presupposes love of oneself as the basis of comparison: "You shall love your neighbour as yourself" (Mk 12:31). Consequently, no one can renounce the right to self-defence out of lack of love for life or for self. This can only be done in virtue of a heroic love which deepens and transfigures the love of self into a radical self-offering, according to the spirit of the Gospel Beatitudes (cf. Mt 5:38-40). The sublime example of this self-offering is the Lord Jesus himself.

Moreover, "legitimate defence can be not only a right but a grave duty for someone responsible for another's life, the common good of the family or of the State". Unfortunately it happens that the need to render the aggressor incapable of causing harm sometimes involves taking his life. In this case, the fatal outcome is attributable to the aggressor whose action brought it about, even though he may not be morally responsible because of a lack of the use of reason.

56. This is the context in which to place the problem of the death penalty. On this matter there is a growing tendency, both in the Church and in civil society, to demand that it be applied in a very limited way or even that it be abolished completely. The problem must be viewed in the context of a system of penal justice ever more in line with human dignity and thus, in the end, with God's plan for man and society. The primary purpose of the punishment which society inflicts is "to redress the disorder caused by the offence". Public authority must redress the violation of personal and social rights by imposing on the offender an adequate punishment for the crime, as a condition for the offender to regain the exercise of his or her freedom. In this way authority also fulfils the purpose of defending public order and ensuring people's safety, while at the same time offering the offender an incentive and help to change his or her behaviour and be rehabilitated.

It is clear that, for these purposes to be achieved, the nature and extent of the punishment must be carefully evaluated and decided upon, and ought not go to the extreme of executing the offender except in cases of absolute necessity: in other words, when it would not be possible otherwise to defend society. Today however, as a result of steady improvements in the organization of the penal system, such cases are very rare, if not practically non-existent.

In any event, the principle set forth in the new Catechism of the Catholic Church remains valid: "If bloodless means are sufficient to defend human lives against an aggressor and to protect public order and the safety of persons, public authority must limit itself to such means, because they better correspond to the concrete conditions of the common good and are more in conformity to the dignity of the human person."

This appendix is an excerpt from Chapter III; the entire encyclical letter is available online, at www.vatican.va/edocs/ENG0141/_INDEX.HTM

Appendix B

Statement By Catholic Bishops Of Texas On Capital Punishment
1997

As spiritual leaders in the community we Catholic Bishops of Texas are acutely aware of the violence in our state. Despite a growing reliance on longer sentences, more prisons, and more executions, our state's crime rate has escalated.

Since the reinstatement of the death penalty in the United States in 1976, the Catholic Bishops of the United States have repeatedly condemned its use as a violation of the sanctity of human life. Capital punishment, along with abortion and euthanasia, is inconsistent with the belief of millions of Texans that all life is sacred.

It is important that we address this issue at this time. Since 1976 Texas has executed more than 100 men, some of whom were mentally retarded or mentally ill. We currently have more than 400 men and women on death row.

We sympathize with the profound pain of the victims of brutal crimes; nevertheless, we believe that the compassionate example of Christ calls us to respect the God-given image found even in hardened criminals.

We must now take bolder steps to change the attitude of the American people regarding capital punishment as a means of dealing with a complex issue. It is unfortunate that a large majority of Americans, including Catholics, support capital punishment as a means of dealing with crime, even in light of strong evidence of its ineffectiveness, its racially-biased application, and its staggering costs, both materially and emotionally.

Capital punishment has not proved to be a deterrent to crime. States which have the death penalty do not have lower rates of violent crime than states without the death penalty. All other western democracies have abolished capital punishment and have lower rates of violent crime.

The imposition of the death penalty has resulted in racial bias. In fact, the race of the victim has been proven to be the determining factor in deciding whether to prosecute capital cases. Of those executed, nearly 90% were convicted of killing whites, although people of color are more than half of all homicide victims in the United States. More than 60% of the persons on death rows in California and Texas are either Black, Latino, Asian, or Native American.

In the State of Texas, it costs $2.3 million on an average to prosecute and execute each capital case as compared to $400,000 for life imprisonment.

Tragically, innocent people are sometimes put to death by the state. It has been proven in 350 capital convictions over the past 20 years that the convicted person had not committed the crime. Of these cases, 25 people were executed before their innocence was discovered.

Capital punishment does nothing for the families of victims of violent crime other than prolonging their suffering through many wasted years of criminal proceedings. Rather than fueling their cry for vengeance, the state could better serve them by helping them come to terms with their grief. We applaud the work of support groups of victims' families who have joined together to work toward reconciliation and rehabilitation of the people who caused tragic loss in their families.

While human logic alone seems to support the abolition of the death penalty, as moral leaders we call for alternatives because of its moral incongruity in today's world. The Catechism of the Catholic Church states, *"If...non-lethal means are sufficient to defend and protect people's safety from the aggressor, authority will limit itself to such means, as these are more in keeping with the concrete conditions of the common good and more in conformity with the dignity of the human person.*

"Today, in fact, as a consequence of the possibilities which the state has for effectively preventing crime, by rendering one who has committed an offense incapable of doing harm—without definitively taking away from him the possibility of redeeming himself—the cases in which the execution of the offender is an absolute necessity are very rare, if not practically nonexistent."

In our modern society, we have means of keeping an offender from harming others. Although in previous times people of faith have employed capital punishment, today we have the ability to realize better the principles of mercy, forgiveness and unconditional love for all people, as evoked in the Hebrew Scriptures by the Prophet Ezekiel: *"As I live, says the Lord GOD, I swear I take no pleasure in the death of the wicked man, but rather in the wicked man's conversion, that he may live. Turn, turn from your evil ways!"*

We believe that capital punishment contributes to a climate of violence in our state. This cycle of violence can be diminished by life imprisonment without parole, when necessary. The words of Ezekiel are a powerful reminder that repentance not revenge, conversion not death are better guides for public policy on the death penalty than the current policy of violence for violence, death for death.

As religious leaders, we are deeply concerned that the State of Texas is usurping the sovereign dominion of God over human life by employing capital punishment for heinous crimes. We implore all citizens to call on our elected officials to reject the violence of the death penalty and replace it with non-lethal means of punishment which are sufficient to protect society from violent offenders of human life and public order.

Appendix C

Good Friday Appeal to End the Death Penalty

A Statement of the Administrative Board of the
United States Conference of Catholic Bishops
April 2, 1999

*The new evangelization calls for followers of Christ who are unconditionally pro-life: who will proclaim, celebrate and serve the Gospel of life in every situation. A sign of hope is the increasing recognition that the dignity of human life must never be taken away, even in the case of someone who has done great evil. Modern society has the means of protecting itself, without definitively denying criminals the chance to reform. I renew the appeal I made most recently at Christmas for a consensus to end the death penalty, which is both cruel and unnecessary.*1
--Pope John Paul II, January 27, 1999, St. Louis, Missouri

For more than 25 years, the Catholic bishops of the United States have called for an end to the death penalty in our land. Sadly, however, death sentences and executions in this country continue at an increasing rate. In some states, there are so many executions they rarely receive much attention anymore. On this Good Friday, a day when we recall our Savior's own execution, we appeal to all people of goodwill, and especially Catholics, to work to end the death penalty.

As we approach the next millennium, we are challenged by the evolution in Catholic teaching on this subject and encouraged by new and growing efforts to stop executions around the world. Through his powerful encyclical, The Gospel of Life (Evangelium Vitae), Pope John Paul II has asked that governments stop using death as the ultimate penalty. The Holy Father points out that instances where its application is necessary to protect society have become "very rare, if not practically nonexistent."2 In January 1999, our Holy Father brought his prophetic appeal to "end the death penalty to the United States, clearly challenging us to "end the death penalty, which is both cruel and unnecessary."3 Our Holy Father has called us with new urgency to stand against capital punishment.

Sadly, many Americans--including many Catholics--still support the death penalty out of understandable fear of crime and horror at so many innocent lives lost through criminal violence. We hope they will come to see, as we have, that more violence is not the answer. However many in the Catholic community are at the forefront of efforts to end capital punishment at state and national levels. Catholics join with others in prayerful witness against executions. We seek to educate and persuade our fellow citizens that this penalty is often applied unfairly and in racially biased ways.[4] We stand in opposition to state laws that would permit capital punishment and federal laws that would expand it.

We strongly encourage all within the Catholic community to support victims of crime and their families. This can be a compassionate response to the terrible pain and anger associated with the serious injury or murder of a loved one. Our family of faith must stand with them as they struggle to overcome their terrible loss and find some sense of peace.

We fully support and encourage these and other efforts to uphold the dignity of all human life. The actions of Catholics who consistently and faithfully oppose the death penalty reflect the call of our bishops' statement Living the Gospel of Life: A Challenge to American Catholics: "Our witness to respect for life shines most brightly when we demand respect for each and every human life, including the lives of those who fail to show that respect for others. The antidote to violence is love, not more violence."[5]

Respect for all human life and opposition to the violence in our society are at the root of our long-standing position against the death penalty. We see the death penalty as perpetuating a cycle of violence and promoting a sense of vengeance in our culture. As we said in Confronting a Culture of Violence: "We cannot teach that killing is wrong by killing."[6]

We oppose capital punishment not just for what it does to those guilty of horrible crimes but for what it does to all of us as a society. Increasing reliance on the death penalty diminishes all of us and is a sign of growing disrespect for human life. We cannot overcome crime by simply executing criminals, nor can we restore the lives of the innocent by ending the lives of those convicted of their murders. The death penalty offers the tragic illusion that we can defend life by taking life.

We are painfully aware of the increased rate of executions in many states. Since the death penalty was reinstituted in 1976, more than 500 executions have taken place, while there have been seventy-four death-row reversals late in the process. Throughout the states, more than 3,500 prisoners await their deaths. These numbers are deeply troubling. The pace of executions is numbing. The discovery of people on death row who are innocent is frightening.

In the spirit of the coming biblical jubilee, we join our Holy Father and once again call for the abolition of the death penalty. We urge all people of good will, particularly Catholics, to work to end the use of capital punishment. At appropriate opportunities, we ask pastors to preach and teachers to teach about respect for all life and about the need to end the death penalty. Through education, through advocacy, and through prayer and contemplation on the life of Jesus, we must commit ourselves to a persistent and principled witness against the death penalty, against a culture of death, and for the Gospel of Life.

---

1. Pope John Paul II, Mass in St. Louis, MO, (January 27, 1999)

2. Pope John Paul II, Evangelium Vitae (The Gospel of Life), par. 56, United States Conference of Catholic Bishops, (1995).

3. Pope John Paul II, Mass in St. Louis, MO, (January 27, 1999).

4. The Death Penalty Information Center, The Death Penalty in Black and White: Who Lives, Who Dies, Who Decides, (June, 1998).

5. United States Conference of Catholic Bishops, (December 3, 1998).

6. United States Conference of Catholic Bishops, Confronting a Culture of Violence: A Catholic Framework for Action, (1994).

Appendix D

Statement on Capital Punishment
Dominican Sisters of Houston, Texas
December 30, 1997

The Dominican Sisters of Houston call for the abolition of the Death Penalty in Texas and throughout the United States.

As women of faith we believe in the sanctity of human life and in the merciful and forgiving God who offers the opportunity for redemption, change and growth.

We stand in solidarity with the Catholic Bishops of Texas, who, in their October, 1997 statement on capital punishment say, 'We implore all citizens to call on our elected officials to reject the Death Penalty and replace it with non-lethal means of punishment which are sufficient to protect society from violent offenders of human life and public order.'

Our compassion goes out to those victims and their families who suffer at the hands of accused and/or convicted criminals. However, we believe that the death penalty is an inappropriate response because it encourages a culture of violence. Furthermore, capital punishment has not proved to be a deterrent to crime.

Appendix E

Corporate Stance on the Abolition of the Death Penalty
Congregation of the Sisters of Charity of the Incarnate Word, Houston, TX
2003

We, the Sisters of Charity of the Incarnate Word, Houston, Texas are called to reverence life in all its forms from conception to natural death. At this time in our history, we see everywhere a growing disregard for the sacredness of human life.

We are challenged to reverence all of life and we declare our opposition to the death penalty.

The United States Catholic Bishops have stated: "Jesus Christ taught us to seek justice with mercy, to love our enemies and to pray for those that persecute us. We add our voice to the public debate on the issue of the death penalty in hopes that we will not harden our hearts in the face of unspeakable violence, but will eventually decide that the best response to violence and death is the biblical call to choose life."

We stand in solidarity with Pope John Paul II, the United States Catholic Conference of Bishops, the Leadership Conference of Women Religious, the Conference of Major Superiors of Men and other Religious traditions who have called for the abolition of the death penalty on religious, moral or humanitarian grounds.

We believe that life in prison without parole is an effective and viable alternative to the death penalty.

We pledge to address the roots of violence, the inequalities in our justice system and call for reform in our prison systems.

Through prayer and support, we will reach out in compassion to families of both victims and perpetrators, supporting them in their loss and pain.

We will work with others to call for an immediate moratorium on the death penalty and do all we can to bring about the abolition of the death penalty in our country.

Appendix F

Resolution Opposing the Death Penalty
Adopted unanimously by the General Assembly of the
Texas Conference of Churches
February 24, 1998

WHEREAS the Texas Conference of Churches, in 1973 and 1977, and many of the churches and judicatories belonging to the Texas Conference of Churches have made clear statements in opposition to and calling for the abolition of the death penalty; and

WHEREAS the Bible does authorize every government to "bear the sword" (Rom. 13:4) and the governments and nations of this world are also called upon to care for "the least of these brothers and sisters" of Christ (Matt. 25:40) thus imposing upon each government and nation the obligation to respond to human situations and crises with justice and mercy; and

WHEREAS Jesus clearly rejected any ideas of "an eye for an eye and a tooth for a tooth," (Matt 5:28-39), and the God of Israel insisted that "Vengeance is mine, I will repay," (Deut. 32:35; and

WHEREAS in our modern society we have means of keeping an offender from harming others. Although in previous times people of faith have employed capital punishment, today we have the ability to realize better the principles of mercy, forgiveness and unconditional love for all people as evoked in the Hebrew Scriptures by the Prophet Ezekiel: "As I live, says the Lord God, I have no pleasure in the death of the wicked, but that the wicked turn from their ways and live; turn back from your evil ways." (Ez. 33:11)* and

WHEREAS the evidence is overwhelming that racism, classism and economics are governing factors in administering the death penalty; and that greater numbers of people of color are executed than is reflected in the general population; that mentally incapacitated people and far too many poor and uneducated people have been executed - thus demonstrating the injustice of the current practice of exercising the death penalty; and

WHEREAS we believe that the compassionate example of Christ calls us to respect the God-given image found even in hardened criminals, and we stand in solidarity with the profound pain of the victims of brutal crime,* therefore be it

RESOLVED that the Texas Conference of Churches in Assembly in San Antonio, February 24, 1998, calls on the State of Texas to put an end to the practice of exercising the death penalty and reaffirms its previous resolutions in 1973 and 1977 in opposition to the death penalty; and be it further

RESOLVED that all judicatories, churches, members and caring citizens acknowledge our complicity in the continuing use of and support of the death penalty. When we are silent in the face of injustice, cruelty or oppression, our silence becomes our assent; and be it further

RESOLVED that we call upon all judicatories, churches, members and caring citizens to work in every way possible to oppose the death penalty and to work to create a humane, just and decent society; and be it further

RESOLVED that copies of this resolution be given publicity within the churches of the Texas Conference of Churches, sent to the Governor of Texas, the Lieutenant-Governor, the Attorney General, to the members of the Texas Legislature, to candidates for these offices and to the Chair of the Texas Board of Pardons and Paroles.

*These paragraphs are quotations from the Statement of the Catholic Bishops on Capital Punishment, October, 1997.

Appendix G

Baptist commission endorses moratorium on death penalty

By Ken Camp
January 13, 2003
Texas Baptist Communications

DALLAS—The Texas Baptist Christian Life Commission has joined the call for a moratorium on the death penalty.

The moral concerns and public policy agency of the Baptist General Convention of Texas voted Jan. 10 to call for a moratorium on capital punishment, declaring the system "unfair" and "broken."

As part of its public policy agenda for the Texas Legislature, the commission also agreed to support legislation that would allow life without parole as a sentencing option for Texas juries.

The commission, underscoring that its role is to speak to Texas Baptists and not for Texas Baptists on moral and ethical issues, also approved an extensive report examining the issue of capital punishment from biblical, historical and social justice perspectives.

The report concludes, "In the final analysis, biblical teaching does not support capital punishment as it is practiced in contemporary society."

Furthermore, the report states, "the practice of capital punishment in our nation and state is an affront to biblical justice, both in terms of its impact on the marginalized in society and in terms of simple fairness. How can we perpetuate a system which is clearly so unfair and so broken?"

The way Texas applies the death penalty is unjust in terms of its impact on racial minorities, the poor, juvenile offenders and inmates who are mistakenly convicted, according to the report.

"Racism in sentencing is not a relic of the past," the report asserts, noting studies that show the race of the victim and the defendant have a direct bearing on sentencing.

The commission's report states that a Texan who murders a white person is five times more likely to be sentenced to death than a Texan who murders an African American. And white Texans rarely receive the death penalty for killing black people.

"Statistically, race is more likely to affect death sentencing than smoking affects the likelihood of dying from heart disease. While the latter evidence has produced significant legal and societal changes, racism continues to be a dominant factor in the administration of the death penalty," the report states.

The commission's report also points to discrimination based on economic class, saying, "A defendant's poverty, lack of firm social standing in the community, and inadequate legal representation at trial or on appeal are all common factors among death-row populations."

The full 52-page Report of the Christian Life Commission of the Baptist General Convention of Texas, *Christians and Capital Punishment*, can be found online at:
www.baptiststandard.com/2003/1_20/pages/death_fulltext.pdf

Appendix H

Extrajudicial, summary or arbitrary executions

Report of the Special Rapporteur on extrajudicial, summary or arbitrary executions, Mr. Bacre Waly Ndiaye, submitted pursuant to Commission resolution 1997/61
Addendum
Mission to the United States of America
22 January 1998

V. CONCLUSIONS AND RECOMMENDATIONS (pages 31-35)

"Where, after all, do universal rights begin? In small places, close to home - so close and so small that they cannot be seen on any maps of the world ... . Unless these rights have meaning there, they have little meaning anywhere. Without concerned citizen action to uphold them close to home, we shall look in vain for progress in the larger world."   Eleanor Roosevelt

A. Concerning the use of the death penalty

140. The Special Rapporteur shares the view of the Human Rights Committee and considers that the extent of the reservations, declarations and understandings entered by the United States at the time of ratification of the ICCPR are intended to ensure that the United States has only accepted what is already the law of the United States. He is of the opinion that the reservation entered by the United States on the death penalty provision is incompatible with the object and purpose of the treaty and should therefore be considered void.

141. Not only do the reservations entered by the United States seriously reduce the impact of the ICCPR, but its effectiveness nationwide is further undermined by the absence of active enforcement mechanisms to ensure its implementation at state level.

142. The Special Rapporteur is of the view that a serious gap exists between federal and state governments, concerning implementation of international obligations undertaken by the United States Government. He notes with concern that the ICCPR appears not to have been disseminated to state authorities and that knowledge of the country's international obligations is almost nonexistent at state level. Further, he is of the opinion that the Federal Government cannot claim to represent the states at the international level and at the same time fail to take steps to implement international obligations accepted on their behalf.

143. The Special Rapporteur is aware of the implications of the United States system of federalism as set out in the Constitution and the impact that it has on the laws and practices of the United States. At the same time, it is clear that the Federal Government in undertaking international obligations also undertakes to use all of its constitutionally mandated powers to ensure that the human rights obligations are fulfilled at all levels.

144. The Special Rapporteur questions the overall commitment of the Federal Government to enforce international obligations at home if it claimed not to be in a position to ensure the access of United Nations experts such as special rapporteurs to authorities at state level. He is concerned that his visit revealed little evidence of such a commitment at the highest levels of the Federal Government.

145. The Special Rapporteur believes that the current practice of imposing death sentences and executions of juveniles in the United States violates international law. He further believes that the reintroduction of the death penalty and the extension of its scope, both at federal and at state level, contravene the spirit and purpose of article 6 of the ICCPR, as well as the international trend towards the progressive restriction of the number of offences for which the death penalty may be imposed. He is further concerned about the execution of mentally retarded and insane persons which he considers to be in contravention of relevant international standards.

146. The Special Rapporteur deplores these practices and considers that they constitute a step backwards in the promotion and protection of the right to life.

147. Because of the definitive nature of a death sentence, a process leading to its imposition must comply fully with the highest safeguards and fair trial standards, and must be in accordance with restrictions imposed by international law. The Special Rapporteur notes with concern that in the United States, guarantees and safeguards, as well as specific restrictions on capital punishment, are not being fully respected. Lack of adequate counsel and legal representation for many capital defendants is disturbing. The enactment of the 1996 Anti-terrorism and Effective Death Penalty Act and the lack of funding of PCDOs have further jeopardized the implementation of the right to a fair trial as provided for in the ICCPR and other international instruments.

148. Despite the excellent reputation of the United States judiciary, the Special Rapporteur observes that the imposition of death sentences in the United States seems to continue to be marked by arbitrariness. Race, ethnic origin and economic status appear to be

key determinants of who will, and who will not, receive a sentence of death. As Justice Marshall stated in Godfrey v. Georgia, "The task of eliminating arbitrariness in the infliction of capital punishment is proving to be one which our criminal justice system - and perhaps any criminal justice system - is unable to perform".

149. The politics behind the death penalty, particularly during election campaigns, raises doubts as to the objectivity of its imposition. The Special Rapporteur believes that the system of election of judges to relatively short terms of office, and the practice of requesting financial contributions particularly from members of the bar and the public, may risk interfering with the independence and impartiality of the judiciary. Further, the discretionary power of the prosecutor as to whether or not to seek the death penalty raises serious concern regarding the fairness of its administration.

150. The process of jury selection may also be tainted by racial factors and unfairness. The Special Rapporteur notes with concern that people who are opposed to or have hesitations about the death penalty are unlikely to sit as jurors and believes that a "death qualified" jury will be predisposed to apply the harshest sentence. He fears that the right to a fair trial before an impartial tribunal may be jeopardized by such juries. Moreover, he is convinced that a "death qualified" jury does not represent the community conscience as a whole, but only the conscience of that part of the community which favours capital punishment.

151. The high level of support for the death penalty, even if studies have shown that it is not as deep as is claimed, cannot justify the lack of respect for the restrictions and safeguards surrounding its use. In many countries, mob killings and lynchings enjoy public support as a way to deal with violent crime and are often portrayed as "popular justice". Yet they are not acceptable in any civilized society.

152. While acknowledging the difficulties that authorities face in fighting violent crime, he believes that solutions other than the increasing use of the death penalty need to be sought. Moreover, the inherent cruelty of executions might only lead to the perpetuation of a culture of violence.

153. The Special Rapporteur is particularly concerned by the current approach to victims' rights. He considers that while victims are entitled to respect and compassion, access to justice and prompt redress, these rights should notbe implemented at the expenses of those of the accused. Courts should not become a forum for retaliation. The duty of the State to provide justice should not be privatized and brought back to victims, as it was before the emergence of modern States.

154. While the Special Rapporteur would hope that the United States would join the movement of the international community towards progressively restricting the use of the death penalty as a way to strengthen the protection of the right to life, he is concerned that, to the contrary, the United States is carrying out an increasing number of executions, including of juveniles and mentally retarded persons. He also fears that executions of women will resume if this trend is not reversed.

155. The Special Rapporteur wishes to emphasize that the use of the death penalty in violation of international standards will not help to resolve social problems and build a more harmonious society but, on the contrary, will contribute to exacerbated tensions between races and classes, particularly at a moment when the United States is proclaiming its intention to combat racism more vigorously.

156. In view of the above, the Special Rapporteur recommends the following to the Government of the United States:

(a) To establish a moratorium on executions in accordance with the recommendations made by the American Bar Association and resolution 1997/12 of the Commission on Human Rights;

(b) To discontinue the practice of imposing death sentences on juvenile offenders and mentally retarded persons and to amend national legislation in this respect to bring it into conformity with international standards;

(c) Not to resume executions of women and respect the de facto moratorium in existence since 1984;

(d) To review legislation, both at federal and state levels, so as to restrict the number of offences punishable by death. In particular, the growing tendency to reinstate death penalty statutes and the increase in the number of aggravating circumstances both at state and federal levels should be addressed in order not to contravene the spirit and purpose of article 6 of the ICCPR and the goal expressed by the international community to progressively restrict the number of offences for which the death penalty is applied;

(e) To encourage the development of public defender systems so as to ensure the right to adequate legal representation for indigent defendants; to reinstate funding for legal resource centres in order to guarantee a more appropriate representation of death row inmates, particularly in those states where a public defender system does not exist. This would also help to diminish the risk of executing innocent persons;

(f) To take steps to disseminate and educate government officials at all levels as well as to develop monitoring and appropriate enforcement mechanisms to achieve full implementation of the provisions of the ICCPR, as well as other international treaties, at state level;

(g) To include a human rights component in training programmes for members of the judiciary. A campaign on the role of juries could further aim at informing the public about the responsibilities of jurors;

(h) To review the system of election of members of the judiciary at state level, in order to ensure a degree of independence and impartiality similar to that of the federal system. It is recommended that in order to provide a greater degree of independence and impartiality that judges be elected for longer terms, for instance 10 years or for life;

(i) In view of the above, to consider inviting the Special Rapporteur on the independence of judges and lawyers to undertake a visit to the United States;

(j) To develop an intensive programme aimed at informing state authorities about international obligations undertaken by the United States and at bringing national laws into conformity with these standards; to increase the cooperation between the Department of Justice and the Department of State to disseminate and enforce the human rights undertakings of the United States;

(k) To lift the reservations, particularly on article 6, and the declarations and understandings entered to the ICCPR. The Special Rapporteur also recommends that the United States ratify the Convention on the Rights of the Child. He further recommends that the United States consider ratifying the first and second Optional Protocols to the ICCPR.

The entire report can be read online, at
www.extrajudicialexecutions.org/reports/E_CN_4_1998_68_Add_3.pdf

Appendix I

Interparliamentary Delegations
Division For Non-European Countries

June 25, 1998

Governor George Bush
State Capitol
Austin, Texas 78711

Dear Governor Bush,

As chairman of the European Parliament's delegation for relations with the United States, I wrote to you some weeks ago in the hope that we might have had the opportunity to meet with you during our visit this week to Texas. While the primary purpose of our visit to Houston is to take part in the 49th EP-US Congress interparliamentary exchange, we are also using the occasion to hold discussions on a variety of issues with prominent Texans. Among other things, we shall be discussing the question of the death penalty in Texas, and it was this matter in particular that we would have liked to talk about directly with you. We are sorry that this will not be possible.

As you know, the European Parliament has been vociferous in its opposition to the death penalty wherever it is applied. Over the years, we have adopted numerous resolutions condemning the practice, which we consider to be both morally wrong and also liable to lead to irreversible miscarriages of justice. At our plenary session last week, Parliament unanimously carried a new resolution calling for a universal moratorium on the death penalty.

The death penalty is either constitutionally outlawed, or its application banned, in all fifteen member states of the European Union, The Council of the European Union, like the Parliament, has frequently expressed its concern at the continued widespread use of the death penalty in the world, particularly by totalitarian states and communist countries such as China and North Korea. At the same time, we have been heartened by the decisions in most of the new democracies in central and Eastern Europe and elsewhere, to abolish the practice.

We are especially saddened to note that in the United States - the world's greatest democracy and proponent of human rights - the number of executions is increasing year by year. Nowhere is this more apparent than in your own State of Texas.

We understand that this is it complex and emotive issue, and I do not propose to rehearse here the arguments that, for us, make legal execution unacceptable under any circumstances. Suffice it to say that we believe the death penalty amounts to retribution rather than deterrence, and that its use always carries with it the risk that an innocent person may die. We understand also that it takes courage to stand above murderers and terrorists and to say: we reject your methods, and we refuse to embrace them as our own.

That said, we are concerned that the almost universal repugnance felt in Europe and elsewhere for the continued application of the death penalty in certain American states may also have economic consequences. Europe is the foremost foreign investor in Texas. Many companies, under pressure from shareholders and public opinion to apply ethical business practices, are beginning to consider the possibility of restricting investment in the U.S. to states that do not apply the death penalty.

I therefore take this opportunity to appeal to you to consider whether the death penalty can honestly constitute a relevant instrument in a modern and compassionate justice system. As Governor, you have the power to commute existing death sentences and to launch a fresh debate in your state about the continued wisdom of applying this extreme form of sanction. I and my colleagues in the European Parliament earnestly hope that you will pause to reflect on the options you have to bring new international respect to your great State and to set an example to the rest of America.

Yours sincerely,

Alan J. Donnelly, MEP
Chairman, Delegation for Relations with the United States

European Union -
Delegation of the European Commission to the United States
2300 M Street, NW, Washington, DC 20037
Telephone: (202) 862-9500 Fax: (202) 429-1766

Appendix J

Vote on a Moratorium on the Use of the Death Penalty
United Nations General Assembly, 27 Dec., 2007

The draft resolution on a moratorium on the use of the death penalty (document A/62/439/Add.2) was adopted by a recorded vote of 104 in favour to 54 against, with 29 abstentions, as follows:

In favour: Albania, Algeria, Andorra, Angola, Argentina, Armenia, Australia, Austria, Azerbaijan, Belgium, Benin, Bolivia, Bosnia and Herzegovina, Brazil, Bulgaria, Burkina Faso, Burundi, Cambodia, Canada, Cape Verde, Chile, Colombia, Congo, Costa Rica, Côte d'Ivoire, Croatia, Cyprus, Czech Republic, Denmark, Dominican Republic, Ecuador, El Salvador, Estonia, Finland, France, Gabon, Georgia, Germany, Greece, Guatemala, Haiti, Honduras, Hungary, Iceland, Ireland, Israel, Italy, Kazakhstan, Kiribati, Kyrgyzstan, Latvia, Liechtenstein, Lithuania, Luxembourg, Madagascar, Mali, Malta, Marshall Islands, Mauritius, Mexico, Micronesia (Federated States of), Moldova, Monaco, Montenegro, Mozambique, Namibia, Nauru, Nepal, Netherlands, New Zealand, Nicaragua, Norway, Palau, Panama, Paraguay, Philippines, Poland, Portugal, Romania, Russian Federation, Rwanda, Samoa, San Marino, Sao Tome and Principe, Serbia, Slovakia, Slovenia, South Africa, Spain, Sri Lanka, Sweden, Switzerland, Tajikistan, The former Yugoslav Republic of Macedonia, Timor-Leste, Turkey, Turkmenistan, Tuvalu, Ukraine, United Kingdom, Uruguay, Uzbekistan, Vanuatu, Venezuela.

Against: Afghanistan, Antigua and Barbuda, Bahamas, Bahrain, Bangladesh, Barbados, Belize, Botswana, Brunei Darussalam, Chad, China, Comoros, Democratic People's Republic of Korea, Dominica, Egypt, Ethiopia, Grenada, Guyana, India, Indonesia, Iran, Iraq, Jamaica, Japan, Jordan, Kuwait, Libya, Malaysia, Maldives, Mauritania, Mongolia, Myanmar, Nigeria, Oman, Pakistan, Papua New Guinea, Qatar, Saint Kitts and Nevis, Saint Lucia, Saint Vincent and the Grenadines, Saudi Arabia, Singapore, Solomon Islands, Somalia, Sudan, Suriname, Syria, Thailand, Tonga, Trinidad and Tobago, Uganda, United States, Yemen, Zimbabwe.

Abstain: Belarus, Bhutan, Cameroon, Central African Republic, Cuba, Democratic Republic of the Congo, Djibouti, Equatorial Guinea, Eritrea, Fiji, Gambia, Ghana, Guinea, Kenya, Lao People's Democratic Republic, Lebanon, Lesotho, Liberia, Malawi, Morocco, Niger, Republic of Korea, Sierra Leone, Swaziland, Togo, United Arab Emirates, United Republic of Tanzania, Viet Nam, Zambia.

Absent: Guinea-Bissau, Peru, Senegal, Seychelles, Tunisia.

APPENDIX K

The Return of Capital Punishment
by Rabbi Samuel M. Stahl

A Temple member approached me several years ago with a request: "Would I address the question of whether a Jew should serve on a jury which imposes the death penalty?" This person then asked: "Do we Jews not believe that God wants sinners to repent and not die?" This question was raised at a time when many states were restoring the death penalty after it had been abolished for many years. The new trend began when Gary Gilmore was executed by a firing squad in Utah in 1977. Our Texas lawmakers, soon thereafter, proposed lethal injections as another way for a government to take a life. Why this swelling support for the death penalty?

In our country we have become increasingly frustrated by the rise in the crime rate. We are aggravated by the failure of our legal system to punish criminals adequately. Many of us also have a pressing desire for revenge, vindictiveness, and retribution. Some have even proposed televising executions. They obviously gain a sadistic delight from such gory spectacle.

The last public hanging took place in Owensboro, Kentucky, in 1936 when a Black man was sent to the gallows. After that, executions were held within the confines of a prison. At the public hanging, in Owensboro, 20,000 people stood on rooftops and telephone poles to witness this barbarism. Before we rush to endorse capital punishment, we should realize that it is often motivated by baser human impulses.

How then have we Jews viewed the death penalty? Of course, our Bible is replete with instances where the death penalty is mandated. If the people of a city turn to idol worship, the city is to be razed and its citizens destroyed. Both a stubborn and rebellious son (*ben sorer umoreh*) and an adulteress were to be stoned to death.

However, later Jewish teachers inform us that these harsh laws were never carried out. They are in the Bible primarily to underscore the gravity and the seriousness of these sins. In fact, the Talmud states that a *Sanhedrin* (Rabbinic legislature) who executes a criminal even once in seventy years is considered cruel.

In that same passage, Rabbi Tarfon and Rabbi Akiba assert that if they had been part of that Sanhedrin, they never would have allowed the execution of a criminal even that infrequently. Their colleague, Shimon ben Gamliel, disagrees with their position and argues for the death penalty. He claims that if such death penalty opponents as Rabbi Tarfon and or Rabbi Akiba would have their way, they would be responsible for the proliferation of murders in Israel. Rabbi Shimon ben Gamliel thus sees capital punishment as deterrent to crime and an effective way to prevent violence and murder.

However, to me, the arguments favoring capital punishment are not compelling. It is not a sound preventive against crime. For example, in England, people were executed in the Middle Ages for picking pockets. Interestingly enough, the crowds who gathered to watch the hanging of pickpockets were favorite targets for pickpockets to do their work.

A sociologist, Karl Levi, conducted a study of "icemen," which is the street name for killers. He discovered that most murderers do not even consider the consequences of their acts of killing. They rarely ponder the possibility of being put to death by the state. A lover may kill his friend, during a spontaneous outburst of anger. An armed robber will often murder because of panic.

Not only is the death penalty ineffective, but, over the years, its chief victims have been members of poor minority communities. The rich and the influential can obtain good defense attorneys and avoid the death penalty. Michael DiSalle, who was once governor of Ohio, found that men on death row had one thing in common: they were penniless. There were other common denominators, as well: low mental ability, little or no education, few friends, and broken homes.

Advocates of the death penalty also overlook the possibility of error. Once the judgment to execute is made and carried out, the result is irrevocable. There is no greater tragedy than the loss of even one human life. We can't correct it even when we later discover that the person was innocent.

There is still another problem with capital punishment. It brutalizes the ones who administer it. A nineteenth-century Vilna rabbi, known as the Netziv, perceived this phenomena in the story of Phinneas, in the Book of Numbers. In this narrative, the men of Israel had engaged in relations with the women of Moab, a pagan tribe. Incest led to idolatry, and the leaders of Israel were hanged.

Soon thereafter, Phinneas, a zealot of God, saw an Israelite man consorting with a woman of Midian, a related pagan tribe. Phinneas pulled out his spear and entered the chamber where they were lying. He thrust his spear into the man and pierced the woman through her belly. God commended Phinneas for his zeal and for averting further calamities to his people.

Then something strange happened. God made a *b'rit shalom*, a covenant of peace, with Phinneas. The Netziv pointed out that, because Phinneas killed, even with the approval of God, he probably would develop a tendancy for more hostile, destructive behavior. God made a covenant for peace with him to assure him of peaceful and gentle behavior in the future.

Thus, we recognize that killing, even on behalf of the state, arouses violence. It cheapens human life. It heightens our need to vent our wrath upon the criminal. It undermines our respect for human life.

Thus we return to our original question: "Should a Jew serve on a jury which inflicts the death penalty?" I believe that, if a Jew does serve on such a jury, he or she should do everything within his or her power to prevent the death sentence from being issued. In Judaism, we see as our goal, the rehabilitation of life, not the destruction of life. Many criminals, with proper counseling and therapy, can be restored to wholesome and productive lives, as we saw in the case of Nathan Leopold.

I believe that if the *Sanhedrin* were functioning today, it would ban the death penalty as contrary to the spirit of Judaism, except in the case of genocidal criminals, like Adolf Eichmann. In fact, both the Reform Central Conference of American Rabbis and the Conservative Rabbinical Assembly of America have condemned it.

The death penalty is outmoded, unspiritual, and ineffective as an instrument of punishment. According to one contemporary Jewish leader, it also "stands in defiance of our efforts to work for a better society through non-violent means."

Reprinted with permission from: **Making the Timeless Timely Thoughts and Reflections of a Contemporary Reform Rabbi,** by Rabbi Samuel M. Stahl, Nortex Press, Austin, TX, 1993. pp. 76-79. Rabbi Stahl is the Rabbi Emeritus of Temple Beth-El in San Antonio, TX.

Appendix L

Homily by The Reverend Emmanuel Charles McCarthy
August 9, 2000, Huntsville, Texas

He Does Not Break the Bruised Reed

"It is God, who is rich in mercy, whom Jesus Christ has revealed as Father."

With these words Pope John Paul II begins what I believe to be the most eternally significant event of his life, namely, the publication of his Encyclical *Dives in Misericordia*, Rich in Mercy. Towards the end of this encyclical the Successor of Peter proclaims that "Mercy [is] the most stupendous attribute of the Creator and Redeemer." Therefore the true God, as opposed to idols conjured up in the human psyche is a God of Holy, Infinite and Everlasting mercy. This is good, good, good news for every human being. In fact, it is the best news any human being could hope for or imagine.

Mercy, of course, need only be given where mercy is needed. Someone consuming a $135.00 meal at the Waldorf Astoria is in no need of the mercy of food, although he or she may be in need of some other corporal manifestation of Divine Mercy.

It is the one person who dies every nine seconds from starvation in the world, the undernourished child whose brain is being irrevocably damaged, the elderly person reduced to eating dog food who are in need of the mercy of bread. Likewise the only people who require the mercy of forgiveness, that is, those who have intentionally harmed us, are those who need forgiveness, that is, those who have intentionally banned us. If someone gives us a two-week, all expenses paid vacation we do not say, "I forgive you." Either we mercifully forgive those who have hurt us or we do not forgive at all.

Amidst all the bombastic Christian oratory heard from the pulpit, the radio, the television and the internet, amidst all the high and low Christian theologizing it is possible for the straightforward commands of Jesus to get lost. Jesus' explicit commission to his disciples in the last paragraph of the Gospel Matthew could not be clearer: Go you therefore and make disciples of all nations, baptizing them in the name of the Father, and of the Son and of the Holy Spirit *and teach them to obey all that I have commanded you*. (Mt 28: 19-20) The explicit conversion command that Jesus teaches also could not be clearer: "I want mercy, not sacrifice." (Mt 9:13) Simpleminded and sophisticated obfuscations and distortions can be concocted to assure that the obvious will never be seen or to assure that what is of primary concern for Jesus is reduced to incidental concern for the billions to whom He has given the gift of faith. But, "I want mercy, not sacrifice" will forever stand in judgment on such intellectual maneuvers and will remain long after "heaven and earth have passed away." Those gifted with faith in Jesus can discount, ignore, modify or rationalize away His teaching in order to advance their interests but His words will forever be there inviting them back: to the truth of the Truth incarnate.

What else could be the truth of Jesus but mercy? If Jesus is as St. Paul says, "the visible image of the invisible God" (Col 1:15), if the God Jesus proclaims is "rich in mercy" (Eph 2:4), if "the Father and I are one" (Jn 10:30), if "he who sees Me sees the Father" (Jn 14:9), then what else could Jesus command other than, "I want mercy, not sacrifice," "Be merciful as your heavenly Father is merciful." (Lk 6:35) Union with the Father who is rich in mercy and communion with Jesus who is the visible image of the invisible God could only be union and communion through, with and in Mercy made flesh.

Mercilessness, regardless of the quality of logic or the cleverness of euphemism by which it perpetuates itself is never of God and is never a part of the economy of salvation. It is mercy that initiates and consummates the process of salvation in Christ. This is why John Paul II writes in *Dives in Misericordia*, "Christ's messianic program of mercy, becomes the program of his people, the program of the Church." This means Christ-like mercy must be the program of each baptized person without any exceptions and without any "time-outs."

"The Church lives an authentic life when she professes and proclaims mercy," proclaims the Pope. Hence, the individual Christian of whatever Church lives an authentic life when he or she professes and proclaims, by thought, word and deed, mercy. The Advocate, the Paraclete, the Public Defender that God sends to this world to act on behalf of human beings is the Spirit of the Father who is rich in mercy, it is the Spirit of the Son who is one with the Father, is the Spirit of the Holy, is the Spirit of Mercy. Satan, literally "the Adversary" of God and humanity, "the Accuser," is ipso facto the spirit of mercilessness.

All mercilessness is then from hell. Indeed, hell is a perpetual state of being merciless: "I was hungry and you did not give me to eat, I was thirsty and you did not give me to drink, I was naked and you did not clothe me. I was in prison and you did not visit me." (Mt 25: 31-46) This teaching of Jesus is the standard of judgment at the end of time. Mercy or mercilessness? It does not require a doctorate from Harvard Divinity School to get this straight. There is something in both the acts of mercy and the acts of mercilessness in time that have radically different consequences in eternity.

Forget the anthropomorphic imagery of devils with pitchforks, etc. Focusing on human images to describe what is beyond individual communal human experience just serves to undermine the seriousness of an eternally life and death problem and mystery. Because of truths we can only get a glimpse of through the revelation of Jesus, we know that indifference to the relievable suffering of another human being, mercilessness, is radical evil. (Mt. 25:46) We also know by this same revelation that responding to the relievable suffering of another human being, mercy, results in entrance into "the Kingdom prepared for you since the foundation of the world." (Mt 25:34)

Providing a person first has faith in Jesus as his/her Lord, God and savior, this makes sense. Jesus reveals to us that God is a Father/Mother/Parent who is rich in mercy.

Reason may be able to tell us God exists but only revelation can tell us God is a Parent rich in mercy. John Paul II in his encyclical says, "Making the Father present as love and mercy is, in Christ's own consciousness, the fundamental touchstone of His mission as the Messiah." Faith in the self-revelation of God in Jesus is preeminent because until one knows what kind of God God is, one cannot know what God expects of those He/She created. A God who is rich in mercy expects of those who wish to be in union with the Divine that they too be rich in mercy. A God who is Father/Mother/Parent of each person expects human beings to relate to each other not as capitalists to communists, not as Americans to Iraqis, not as haves to have-nots, not as Croats to Serbs, not as the righteous to the sinners, not as Pilate to Jesus, but as brothers and sisters endeavoring to assist each other in being merciful as Christ is merciful, in being merciful as their Father in heaven in merciful, in being helpers of one another on The Way of Mercy that leads to eternal life for one and all.

In *Dives in Misericordia* the Pope says that, "Mercy constitutes the fundamental content of the messianic message of Christ and the constitutive power of his mission."

Now if mercy is the essential power of Jesus' mission, if mercy is His conversion demand, if mercy is the standard of judgment at the end of the world, if mercy is the most stupendous attribute of the Creator and Redeemer, is it possible that a Christian, someone who truly has faith in Jesus as their Lord, God and Savior, would cast aside mercy even if he or she could gain the whole world or some paltry piece thereof? Would it not be irrational in the extreme for a believer in Christ to even entertain such a thought? Would it not be tragic unseriousness to engage in un-Christ-like mercilessness and then pacify one's soul by renaming mercilessness "mercy," by renaming the Satanic the Christic?

"If our hopes in Christ are limited to this life only, we are the most pitiable of people," says St. Paul (I Cor. 15:19) For the Christian to live in time as if eternity does not exist is intrinsically absurd. For a Christian to choose mercilessness rather than mercy, in order to gain the totally perishable, is insanity.

Fifty-eight years ago today, on August 9, 1942, in total conformity with all the laws of the German government of the time, Christians gassed St. Edith Stein to death at Auschwitz. Fifty-seven years ago today, on August 9, 1943, at Brandenburg Prison and in total conformity with the laws of the German government of the time, Christians on behalf of the state beheaded Franz Jäggerstätter, the only Austrian layman who was a conscientious objector to being conscripted into Hitler's army. Fifty-five years ago today, on August 9, 1945, in total conformity with the laws of the United States government at the time, an entirely Christian bomb crew on behalf of the State dropped the atomic bomb on Nagasaki – the oldest, original and largest Christian community in all Japan. And today, August 9, 2000, in total conformity with the laws of the United States Government, Christians on behalf of the State of Texas poisoned to death two of their brothers in Christ – Oliver Cruz and Brian Roberson.

The state laws under which Christians destroyed each of these Christians can be accredited or discredited depending on one's use of reason. What reason builds up, reason can tear down. But what cannot be denied is the overt Christian mercilessness in each situation. What cannot be denied is that the spirit that entered history through Cain and did its most horrific work on Calvary is the same spirit that killed Edith Stein, Franz Jäggerstätter, the people of Nagasaki, Oliver Cruz and Brian Roberson. Is it the same spirit that acted through Mr. Cruz and Mr. Roberson if they killed other human beings?

You bet it is! Is it the spirit that is the Adversary of mercy? You bet it is! It is the perverted and perverting spirit of mercilessness, manifested as homicidal violence that is at the root of all this destruction.

God is a Father/Mother/Parent rich in mercy. God forgives. God forgives 70x7 times which is why the disciples of Jesus are told to be mercifully forgiving 70x7 times.

How total, how complete is God's forgiving mercy? The publican is so spiritually distraught that he cannot even raise his eyes in the back of the synagogue. All he can do is look down and strike his breast and pray, "O God be merciful to me a sinner." (Lk 18:13) Jesus says of him, "I assure you, that man goes away justified." (Lk 18:14) How total, how complete is God's forgiving mercy? The thief on the cross next to Jesus is so full of self hate he thinks deserves death. Then, for the only time in the Gospels, Jesus is addressed directly by his proper name, "Jesus, remember me when you come into your Kingdom." (Lk 23:42) Jesus, the incarnation of the true God, the God who is rich in mercy, bestows on this so-called "no-gooder," that the politically and religiously powerful of this world feel this world would be better off without, mercy on a scale unbeknownst in prior human history: "I assure you; this day you will be with me in paradise." (Lk 23-43) We could go on with the Prodigal Son and with "Father forgive them for they know not what they do" but the point is self-evident: God's mercy, the mercy Christians are called to imitate, is a superabundant mercy. It is never begrudging or stingy. It never proceeds from obligation. It always issues from generosity. It is always a gift. John Paul II wrote in his encyclical that "[T]he genuine face of mercy has to ever be revealed anew."

Was the Face of God, the Face of Mercy, revealed today, August 9, 2000, at Huntsville Prison? At Auschwitz on August 9, 1942? At Brandenburg Prison on August 9, 1943? Or was Christianity, in each case, used as a mask to hide the face of the diabolical? The blood on Jesus' hands is His own. Capital punishment is not what Jesus taught, it is what Jesus suffered. Crucifying, gassing, beheading, handing, shooting, electrocuting and poisoning people are not the works of mercy. The God who is rich in mercy is never glorified by homicidal violence. "Praise the Lord and pass the ammunition," or "Praise the Lord and fire up 'ole Sparky," or "Praise the Lord and turn on the gas," or "Praise the Lord and release the poison" are blasphemy and falsehood.

Their source is the "Father of lies who is a murderer from the beginning" and not the "Father who is rich in mercy." These are the works and words of the Adversary of mercy, the Adversary of Christ.

If Jesus is only a philosopher, then rejecting the risks of mercy in favor of power, pleasure, nationalism, religionism, comfort, etc. is a rational option. But, if Jesus is the definitive revelation of God and God's will to humanity, then rejecting risks of mercy is spiritual suicide.

No one is sinless, but all are sacred. No one is going to come to his or her last breath saying, "God have justice on me!" But if it is mercy we want in eternity, is it not mercy we should give in time? "Forgive us our trespasses as we forgive those who trespass against us" is either meaningless babble into infinite emptiness or it is a request that God judges us as we have judged others. Jesus says, "Blessed are the merciful for they shall obtain mercy." (Mt. 5:7) And, what does He say the fruits of mercilessness will be? (Mt 25:45-46; Lk 16:19)

Christians must cease endorsing and participating in capital punishment because it is incontestably incompatible with following the Nonviolent Jesus of the Gospels and His Way of nonviolent love of friends and enemies. Christians must cease advocating and justifying capital punishment because it is in direct violation of that commandment of Jesus which the New Catechism of the Catholic Church (sec 1970) says contains the entire law of the Gospel: "I gave you a new commandment, love one another as I have loved you." (Jn 13:34; Jn 15:12) As Jesus cannot be pictured burning witches at the stake, He equally cannot be pictured gassing, shooting, guillotining, electrocuting, poisoning or crucifying human beings. What Christians cannot picture Christ doing, they are forbidden to do. Christians must cease all active support of capital punishment because by their support they bear false witness to other Christians and to non-Christians and thereby become obstacles to people coming to Jesus and knowing the true God. By bearing false witness such Christians, who were chosen to be agents of the healing power of Jesus Christ become instead major hindrances to Jesus healing the pandemic of organized mercilessness that is spreading throughout the world. Finally, Christians regardless of rank, status, class or occupation must abandon capital punishment because they were created from Mercy for Mercy and in Jesus they have been granted the gift of knowing that the way to Mercy Eternal is by the way of Mercy in Time.

Let us leave with a final thought from the August 9 victim of capital punishment, St. Edith Stein: "It is mercy that makes us one with God."

Let us pray:
  Mary, Mother of Jesus, mother of a victim of the merciless spirit of homicidal violence and Mother of Mercy, intercede with your violated Jesus for the victims of violence, intercede with your victimized Son for deep peace for the loved ones of the victims of violence and intercede with your forgiving Son who on the cross prayed, "Father forgive them for they know not what they do," for the executioners of violence. In your compassion, pray to your fair Child, the Suffering Servant, that all His disciples learn from Him how to live without breaking "the bruised reed." (Is. 42:3) Amen.

Appendix M

October 14, 2004

Texas Board of Pardons and Paroles
Austin, Texas

Dear Sir:

I am writing in reference to the case of Dominique Green who is scheduled to be executed on October 26, 2004. I understand that a clemency petition has been filed to have Mr. Green's death sentence commuted to a life sentence. I would like to have this letter considered as part of your decision in this issue. As the widow of Andrew Lastrapes, I feel like I have been affected by this crime more than any other person, with the exception of my two sons, Andre and Andrew.

The loss of my husband, Andrew, was devastating to me and my family. However, I don't believe that Dominique should have received the death penalty. He came from an very abusive family situation. His mother was mentally ill and did not help him at all during his trial. In fact, I saw her sleeping on the bench at the trial! Dominique's father did not help either – he was nowhere to be seen.

I was especially disturbed at the trial that the white boy involved in the crime did not spend any time in jail. And yet Dominique received the death penalty! Where is the justice in that? There was something very, very wrong with what happened in that trial in my opinion.

Andrew Lastrapes and I had two sons, Andre and Andrew, who both live with me in Houston. Both Andre and Andrew feel as I do. They do not want to see Dominique executed.

God teaches us that we should forgive one another as he has forgiven us. All of us have forgiven Dominique for what happened and want to give him another chance at life. Everyone deserves another chance!

You would honor the memory of my husband, Andrew Lastrapes, by commuting the sentence of Dominique Green to life. For the love of God and justice, please commute his sentence to life.

Sincerely,

Bernatte Lastrapes

Bernatte Luckett Lastrapes

Letter from Bernatte Lastrapes; her son, Andre Lastrapes (right) visited with Dominique Green just before the execution on October 26, 2004. Andre said, *"Killing him ain't going to bring my daddy back."*

Appendix N

Index of Court Cases

These legal citations are included for those persons interested in conducting further research on the individuals and their cases referred to in court opinions.

Randall Dale Adams, *Adams v. State*, 577 S.W.2d 717 (Tex. Cr. App. 1979); *Ex parte Adams*, 768 S.W.2d 281 (Tex. Cr. App); *Adams v. Texas*, 448 U.S. 38 (1980)

Clarence Brandley, *Ex Parte Brandley*, 781 S.W.2d 886 (Tex. Cr. App. 1989)

Ricardo Aldape Guerra, *Guerra v. Johnson*, 90 F.3d 1075 (5th Cir. 1996), *Guerra v. State*, 771 S.W.2d 453 (Tex. Cr. App.1988).

Kerry Max Cook , *Cook v. State*, reversed, without comment, (Tex. Cr. App., March 19, 1997)

Ernest Willis, 27,787-0, (Tex. Cr. App. 2000). *Willis v. Cockrell*, 2004 WL 1812698 (W.D. Tex. 2004)

Richard Wayne Jones, *Jones v State*, 843 S.W.2d 487 (Tex. Cr. App 1992)

Odell Barnes Jr., *Barnes v. State*, 876 S.W.3d 316 (Tex. Cr. App. 1994)

Gary Lee Graham (Shaka Sankofa) *Graham v. State*, 913 S.W.2d 745 (Tex. Cr. App. 1996); *Graham v. Collins*, 950 F.2d 1009 (5th Cir. 1992); *Graham v. Johnson*, 94 F.3d 958 (5th Cir. 1996); *Graham v. Johnson*, 168 F.3d 762 (5th Cir. 1999).

Ruben Montoya Cantu, *Cantu v. State*, 738 S.W.2d 249 (Tex. Cr. App. 1987). *Cantu v. Johnson*, 967 F.2d 1006 (5th Cir. 1992).

Carlos DeLuna, *DeLuna v. State*, 711 S.W. 2d 44 (Tex. Cr. App 1986).

Cameron Todd Willingham, *Willingham v. State*, 897 S.W.2d 351(Tex. Cr. App. 1995).

Johnny Paul Penry, *Penry v. Lynaugh*, 492 U. S. 302 (1989);*Penry v. State*, 903 S.W.2d 715 (Tex. Cr. App. 1995); *Penry v. Texas*, 515 U. S. 1304 (1995); *Penry v. Johnson*, 532 U. S. 782 (2001)

Larry Keith Robison, *Robison v. Texas*, 888 S.W.2d 473 (Tex. Cr. App. 1994).

Dominque Jerome Green, *Green v. State*, 906 S.W.2d 937 (Tex. Cr. App 1995); *Green v. State*, 934 S.W.2d 92 (Tex. Cr. App 1996) and *Green v. Dretke*, 82 Fed. Appx. 333 (5th Cir. 2003).

Mario Marquez, *Marquez v. Collins*, 11 F.3d. 1241 (5th Cir. 1994)

Anthony Ray Westley, *Westley v. State*, 754 S.W.2d 224 (Tex. Cr. App 1988).

Joseph John Cannon, *Cannon v. State*, 691 S.W.2d 664 (Tex. Cr. App. 1985), *Cannon v. Johnson*, 134 F.3d 683 (5th Cir. 1998).

Jonathan Wayne Nobles, *Nobles v. State*, 843 S.W.2d 503 (Tex. Cr. App. 1992).

Glen Charles McGinnis, *McGinnis v. Johnson*, 98-20375 (5th Cir. 1999).

David Oliver Cruz, *Cruz v. State*, 71,004, slip op. (Tex. Cr. App. 1993) *Cruz v. Texas*, 513 U.S. 965 (1994). *Ex parte Cruz*, No. 89-CR-1732A-W1 (Tex. Dist. Ct. 1997), *Ex parte Cruz*, No. 29,545-05 (Tex. Cr. App. 1997). *Cruz v. Johnson*, SA-98-132-FB (W.D. Tex. 1999).

Brian Keith Roberson, *Roberson v. Texas*, 93-5585, 510 U.S. 966 (1993).

Craig Neil Ogan Jr., *Ogan v. Cockrell*, 297 F.3d 349 (5th Cir. 2002).

James Vernon Allridge III, *Allridge v. State*, 850 S.W.2d 471 (Tex. Cr. App. 1991), *Allridge v. Cockrell*, 92 Fed.Appx. 60 (5th Cir. 2003).

Anthony Guy Fuentes, *Fuentes v. State*, 991 S.W.2d 267 (Tex. Cr. App. 1999); *Fuentes v. Texas*, 528 U.S. 1026 (1999); *Fuentes v. Dretke*, 89 Fed.Appx. 868 (5th Cir. 2004).

Joseph Stanley Faulder, *Faulder v. State*, 611 S.W.2d 630 (Tex. Cr. App. 1979); *Faulder v. Johnson*, 178 F.3d 741 (5th Cir. 1999).

Irineo Montoya Tristan, *Tristan v. Scott*, 65 F.3d 405 (5th Cir. 1995).

Jose Ernesto Medellin, *Ex parte Medellin*, Order, No. 50191-01 (Tex. Cr. App. 1997); *Medellin v. Johnson*, 371 F.3d 270, (5th Cir. 2005); *Medellin v. Texas*, 544 U.S. 660 (2008).

Dennis Zelaya (Carlos Manuel Ayestas), *Ayestas v. State*, 72,928 (Tex. Cr. App. 1998) unpublished.

Heliberto Chi, *Chi v. State*, No. 74,492, slip. op. at 3-5 (Tex. Cr. App. 2004).

Karla Faye Tucker, *Tucker v. State*, 771 S.W.2d 523 (Tex. Cr. App. 1988).

Thomas Miller El, *Miller-El v. State*, 748 S.W.2d. 459 (Tex. Cr. App. 1988); *Miller-El v. Texas*, 537 U.S. 322 (2003).

Napolean Beazley, *Beazley v. Texas*, No. 72,101 (Tex. Cr. App. 1997) (unpublished); *Ex parte Beazley*, Writ No. 36,151-01 (Tex. Cr. App. 1998) (unpublished), *Beazley v. Johnson*, 242 F.3d 248 (5th Cir. 2001).

Stacey Lamont Lawton, *Lawton v. State*, 913 S.W.2d 542 (Tex. Cr. App. 1995).

Tony Neyshea Chambers, *Chambers v. Johnson*, 99-40896, (5th Cir 2000).

James Blake Colburn, *Colburn v. State* , 966 S.W.2d 511 (Tex. Cr. App. 1998).

Kelsey Patterson, *Patterson v. Dretke*, 2004 WL 1091998, 370 F.3d 480 (5th Cir. 2004).

Scott Louis Panetti, *Panetti v. Quarterman*, 127 S. Ct. 2842 (June 2007).

Andrea Pia Yates, *Yates v. State*, 171 S.W.3d 215 (Tex. App.—Houston [1st Dist.] 2005).

Appendix O

Suggestions for Further Reading

Adams, Randall D., *Adams vs. Texas*. St. Martin's Press, 1991.

Bedau, Hugo A., ed. *The Death Penalty in America: Current Controversies*. Oxford University Press, 1997.

Cheever, Joan M., *Back from the Dead: One Woman's Search for the Men Who Walked Off America's Death Row*. John Wiley & Sons Ltd, 2006.

Cook, Kerry Max. *Chasing Justice: My Story of Freeing Myself After Two Decades on Death Row for a Crime I Didn't Commit*. William Morrow, 2007.

Davies, Nick. *White Lies: Rape, Murder, and Justice Texas Style*. Pantheon, 1991.

Dow, David R., *Executed on a Technicality: Lethal Injustice on America's Death Row*. Beacon Press, 2005.

Houle, Kristin, *Mental Illness and the Death Penalty Resource Guide*, September, 2007 available online at <www.tcadp.org/uploads/documents/midp%20resource%20guide2.pdf> or by calling 512-441-1808.

King, Rachel. *Don't Kill in Our Names: Families of Murder Victims Speak Out Against the Death Penalty*. Rutgers University Press, 2003.

Lifton, Robert J. and Mitchell, Greg. *Who Owns Death? Capital Punishment, the American Conscience and the End of Executions*. William Morrow, 2000.

Marquart, James, Ekland-Olson, Sheldon and Sorensen, James. *The Rope, The Chair, and The Needle: Capital Punishment in Texas, 1923-1990*. University of Texas, 1994.

Megivern, James J., *The Death Penalty: An Historical and Theological Survey*. Paulist Press, 1997.

Pickett, Carrol and Carlton Stowers. *Within These Walls: Memoirs of a Death House Chaplain*. St. Martin's Press, 2002.

Prejean, Helen. *Dead Man Walking: An Eyewitness Account of the Death Penalty in the United States*. Random House, 1993

Radelet, Michael L., Bedau, Hugo A. and Putnam, Constance E. *In Spite of Innocence: Erroneous Convictions in Capital Cases*. Northeastern, 1994.

Recinella, Dale, *The Biblical Truth about America's Death Penalty*. Northeastern, 2004.

Sarat, Austin. *When the State Kills: Capital Punishment and the American Condition*. Princeton University Press, 2001.

Scheck, Barry, Neufield, Peter and Dwyer, Jim. *Actual Innocence: Five Days to Execution, and Other Dispatches From the Wrongly Convicted.* Doubleday, 2000.

Von Drehle, David. A*mong the Lowest of the Dead: The Culture on Death Row.* Crown, 1995.

Recommended Web sites

Death Penalty Information Center: www.deathpenaltyinfo.org
National Coalition to Abolish the Death Penalty: www.ncadp.org
Amnesty International: www.amnestyusa.org/abolish/
Death Penalty News/Updates: http://people.smu.edu/rhalperi/
Texas Coalition to Abolish the Death Penalty: www.tcadp.org
Catholic Campaign to End the death Penalty: www.ccedp.org
Texas Defender Service: www.texasdefender.org
Texas Catholic Campaign to End the Death Penalty:
www.txccedp.org

Appendix P
Clips From David Atwood's Archives

clockwise, from upper left: Protest outside the office of the Harris County District Attorney during the 1997 NCADP conference; Protest ouside the Walls Unit, Huntsville; Protesting the execution of Karla Faye Tucker, Feb. 1998.

Clockwise, from top left: Lois Robison's mentally-ill son Larry was executed; Rubin "Hurricane" Carter pleading for Joseph Faulder's life, in 1998; Demonstration in Houston during President Clinton's Town Meeting on Race and Sports, 1998; Arianna Ballotta, president of the Italian Coalition to Abolish the Death Penalty and David Atwood speak at the Texas Capitol.

Above: The Westley family and David Atwood outside the Walls Unit in Huntsville at Anthony Westley's execution, Aug. 1997 Below: Sr. Helen Prejean leads a march in San Antonio, June, 1998

Date_____

Dear Members of the Texas Board of Pardons and Paroles,

I urge you to commute the death sentence of Napoleon Beazley, who is scheduled to be executed at 6 PM on May 28, 2002.

This plea does not diminish or excuse the murder of John Luttig. However, I believe that justice can be served without executing Napoleon, who was only 17 years old at the time of the offense.

The United Nations has stated that it "deplores" execution of juvenile offenders. Essentially every nation in the world has abandoned the practice. In the last nine years, only three states within the United States have executed juvenile offenders, while presently 28 bar it by law.

Please help Texas maintain universally accepted human rights norms by granting Napoleon clemency.

    Sincerely,
(Return Address)
_____
_____
_____

TO: Texas Board of Pardons & Paroles
     Executive Clemency Division
     P.O. Box 13401, Capitol Station
     Austin, Texas 78711

Photo Copyright 2002 Texas Monthly,
O. Rufus Lovett

Postcards such as this one asking for clemency in the case of Napoleon Beazley are distributed by TCADP.

Top Ten Reasons to Abolish the Death Penalty

PARTNERS IN CRIME

10. Executions are immoral and evil
9. Executions are reserved for the poor who cannot hire their own attorneys
8. State killings brutalize society causing more murder and mayhem
7. Innocent people are sentenced to death
6. Executions are more costly than life in prison
5. Why do we kill people who kill people to show that killing is wrong?
4. Murder rates are lower in states that have abolished the death penalty
3. The death penalty is racist
2. Every western democracy except the USA has abolished the death penalty
1. The death penalty is uncivilized

TCADP flier, designed by Jimmy Dunne.

Johnny Paul Penry, whose IQ is estimated to be between 53 and 60, spent most of his days on death row drawing with crayons. He came within four hours of being executed before the U.S. Supreme Court intervened.

James Allridge was clearly one of the most accomplished artists on death row. His wonderful drawings of flowers and animals were seen by people throughout the world. He was executed on August 26, 2004.

Huntsville Item, Aug. 24, 2004

Allridge execution unnecessary

To the Editor:

A good friend of mine on Texas death row, James Allridge III, is about to be executed on Aug. 26. James is probably the most rehabilitated man I have ever met on the row. When you visit with him, his creative spirit shines through. You feel you are in the presence of a fully-developed human being. I would not hesitate to have Allridge live with me and my family if he was ever to be released from prison.

Allridge committed a terrible crime many years ago when he murdered Brian Clendennen during a robbery. He caused the Clendennen family pain and suffering that most of us cannot comprehend. Allridge is repentant for what he did and has apologized to the family. While an apology does not make up for having a loved one taken from you, it does indicate that Allridge has taken full responsibility for what he did. Allridge is not seeking to be released, but only to have his death sentence commuted to life in prison.

Allridge will probably be executed unless the Texas Board of Pardons and Paroles (TBPP) and Gov. Perry intervene. If they do intervene, it will have to be on the basis that Allridge is rehabilitated and is a different person than the one who committed a terrible crime many years ago.

In Texas, one reason that people who commit capital murder get the death penalty rather than a life sentence is that they are deemed to be a "future danger to society." Allridge's exemplary life in prison has shown that the jury that made that decision in his case was wrong. That is enough reason for the TBPP and the governor to commute Allridge's death sentence to life in prison.

DAVID ATWOOD
Houston

Editor's note: Allridge was executed Thursday night in Huntsville just a couple of hours after the U.S. Supreme Court rejected a last-second appeal.

Conroe Courier, Jul. 3, 2002

To the editor:

I could not disagree more with The Courier editorial of June 21 (High court oversteps on execution ruling).

The U.S. Supreme Court did all of us a huge favor by ruling against the execution of people with mental retardation. Only the most right-wing, pro-death penalty newspaper would see it differently.

The Supreme Court ruling reflects the desires of not only the American people, but also the citizens of Texas. In the last legislative session, both houses of the Texas government passed a bill that would stop the execution of mentally retarded people. Gov. Perry, in his desire to please his right-wing supporters, vetoed the bill.

So when The Courier states that "Texas was in the throes of deciding this issue for itself," the reality is that Texas did decide this issue through its legislators, but our right-wing governor decided not to go along with the citizens.

**David Atwood
Houston**

Houston Chronicle, March 8, 2000

Regarding the Feb. 27 editorial "Gravitas": For a pro-death penalty newspaper which has supported George W. Bush for governor, the Chronicle reached a new low by suggesting that Bush's record on executions somehow makes him qualified for president.

Remember, Bush is the man who mocked Karla Fay Tucker last year saying, "Please don't kill me." How is that for "gravitas"? Thanks to Bush, Texas has the reputation as being the "death penalty capital of the Western world." In fact, Texas has had so many executions that a Chicago newspaper labeled the state a "serial killer" a few years ago.

Bush is not qualified to be president, but he might be a good candidate for "Lord High Executioner" of the United States.

Dave Atwood, Houston

LETTERS FROM OUR READERS

Another murder in Texas?

To the Editor:

James Allridge was executed on Aug. 26 for the murder of Brian Clendennen in Ft. Worth many years ago. This was the 325th execution in Texas since the death penalty was resumed in the state in 1982. We have about 450 people on our death row and 10 more executions scheduled before the end of the year.

Allridge caused Clendennen and his family horrific pain and suffering that most of us can't comprehend. However, by executing Allridge, we created another set of victims, the Allridge family, who now have experienced the same horrific pain and suffering as the Clendennen family. Both families deserve our prayers and support.

I was one of six witnesses for Allridge during the execution. Allridge included me because I had been visiting him on death row for many years. Personally, I have never experienced anything so evil in all my life — strapping a live human being to a gurney and pumping poison into his veins. I felt like I was in Nazi Germany.

Allridge was a rehabilitated person who had become an accomplished artist and writer while in prison. He was remorseful for the crime he committed as a young man many years ago. His execution was senseless and satisfied no valid societal goal. He was a model prisoner and mentor for other prisoners on death row. If given a life sentence and placed in the prison's general population, he could have been a very positive influence on other prisoners.

However, his execution sends a strong message that rehabilitation and good behavior are, in the long run, not important to the State of Texas.

Allridge's execution will not bring true closure or healing to the family of Brian Clendennen. They will always have a painful wound. Only love and forgiveness can bring a semblance of peace. Allridge's execution will not deter other crimes or make us a better, safer society. We would be better off addressing the root causes of crime such as child abuse and neglect, mental disabilities and negative peer pressure rather than putting so much energy and money into the death penalty, which is truly a false solution to crime.

DAVID ATWOOD
Houston

Huntsville item, May, 9, 2004

Texas Catholic Herald, Dec. 19, 2003

what's wrong with texas?

While the Texas execution machinery relentlessly puts people to death (5 executions scheduled in December alone), the rest of the world looks on with amazement.

I learned this recently while participating in a program in Italy with Ross Byrd, son of James Byrd, Jr., who was murdered in Jasper, Texas, in 1998. Ross has come out against the death penalty for the men who murdered his father and actually visited one of them in prison.

Ross had an opportunity to express his opposition to the death penalty during a program called Cities for Life, Cities Against the Death Penalty, sponsored by the Sant' Egidio Community in Rome, Italy, on November 30. Over 125 cities throughout the world illuminated a monument or important building that evening as an expression of opposition for the death penalty. Those cities included Rome, Berlin, Amsterdam, Tokyo, Santiago, Vienna, Madrid, Brussels, Bogota, Stockholm and San Salvador. In Texas, Catholic Cathedrals were illuminated in Houston, Austin, Dallas, Ft. Worth, El Paso and Victoria.

Ross was also able to participate in the 4th World Summit of the Nobel Peace Prize Laureates, hosted by Mikhail Gorbachev. During this conference, the Nobel Peace Laureates issued a statement which said, "We appeal to the governments of the world to stop all executions and to search for better instruments of justice, defense of human life and human dignity."

A common question addressed to both Ross and myself was this: If a young African-American man whose father was brutally murdered by three racists in Texas was able to speak out against the execution of those men, what is wrong with the rest of Texas? A good question for all of us.

David Atwood
Houston, TX

Houston Chronicle, Nov. 2003

Third jury option is only fair

Regarding the Nov. 28 Chronicle Metropolitan article, "Lawmakers pitch new choice for juries: life without parole": It was disingenuous for retiring Harris County District Attorney John B. Holmes Jr. to argue against a life-without-parole option in capital cases by implying that it would: (1) eliminate all death sentences; (2) cost taxpayers more than executions; and (3) result in prison overcrowding.

Providing a life-without-parole option has not resulted in the elimination of death sentences in other states.

Regarding the cost, a 1992 study indicated that the average cost of an execution then was $2.3 million — three times the cost of life imprisonment.

Texas should conduct an updated study of the costs associated with each option.

Texas' death row houses about 450 inmates, compared to about 160,000 inmates in the entire prison system.

If we are going to need more geriatric prison housing, it won't be due to giving juries a life-without-parole option.

It is just and prudent to provide juries with this third option — protective of society, but which does not result in death.

David Atwood, Houston

Continuing death penalty is only bad for Texas

By DAVID ATWOOD

THE year 2002 was a banner year for Texas and the death penalty. There were 33 executions in Texas, almost 50 percent of all the executions in the United States. This included three juvenile offenders, all of whom were black. Of the 21 juvenile offenders executed in the United States since the death penalty was reinstated in the mid-1970s, 13 have been in Texas alone.

Certain district attorneys and politicians are proud of this record. However, none of these people has made the case that these executions are good for Texas. They can't, because the death penalty is bad for Texas. Despite the high number of executions over the past five years, Texas saw an increase in its homicide rate in 2001.

This is not surprising, however, since most criminal justice experts agree that murder rates depend on such factors as demographics, economics, the drug trade and community policing, but not the death penalty.

Texas will crank up its execution machinery with a bang starting this month. Seven executions are planned in January alone, and five more are scheduled in February. Texas, which reinstated the death penalty in 1982, may hit 300 executions in late February or early March. Another opportunity for the pro-death penalty folks to celebrate.

If recent reports by the Texas Defender Service are correct, and I believe they are, many of the people scheduled for execution in 2003 should not be on death row. Many experienced inadequate legal defense because they were poor. Some experienced racism. Some are mentally disabled. And some may be innocent. The claim by prosecutors that each defendant has had his case thoroughly reviewed in the courts is simply not accurate when one considers the poor legal representation that many defendants have received. Changes in the laws in the mid-1990s have made it more difficult to bring up constitutional issues during the appeals process.

Furthermore, we should not forget that the Texas Court of Criminal Appeals has a record of declaring many serious errors in the trial court (e.g., sleeping lawyers, racism during sentencing) as "harmless errors."

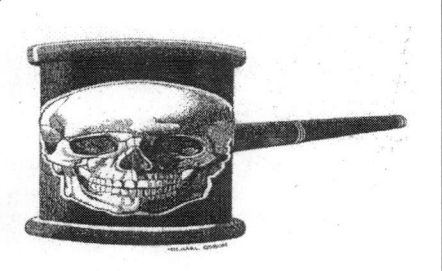

Atwood, a Houstonian, is a member of the Texas Coalition to Abolish the Death Penalty

Texas has an opportunity to remedy many of the deficiencies in its death penalty process during the next legislative session, which starts this month. However, this may not happen considering the makeup of the Legislature after the last election and Gov. Rick Perry's propensity to side with the pro-death penalty crowd.

It is a well-known fact that many conservative legislators and district attorneys will resist improvements to the system and may even try to expand the death penalty. In fact, there will probably be an effort to water down and make ineffective the latest U.S. Supreme Court ruling that bars the execution of people with mental retardation.

If conservative legislators and district attorneys resist meaningful improvements in the criminal justice system, that will be bad for Texas in a number of ways.

- First, people who should not be on death row will end up there.
- Secondly, the system will continue to discriminate against the poor, minorities and people with mental disabilities.
- Thirdly, some innocent people may be executed.
- Fourthly, money that could be used for effective crime prevention methods will continue to be wasted on the death penalty.
- Finally, Texas' reputation as the "Death Penalty Capital of the Western World" will continue to grow throughout the world.

Wouldn't we prefer that our worldwide reputation be based on something other than the death penalty? How about excellence in health care, education and business opportunities?

All things considered, it would be best for Texas to get rid of the death penalty altogether. Twelve states do not have the death penalty and seem to be doing fine. In fact, Michigan has not had the death penalty in over 150 years. Other states that have the death penalty on the books rarely use it.

The truth is that the death penalty is not needed for societal protection. Long-term incarceration can fulfill that need. We can be "tough on crime" without killing people. And the families of murder victims will be better off because they can get on with their lives rather than waiting for an execution that does not give them the closure they desire.

Outlook

Items on this page do not necessarily reflect the opinions of the Houston Chronicle

Time we turn Texas into a truly civilized state

By DAVE ATWOOD

THE execution on Wednesday of Javiar Suarez Medina, a citizen of Mexico, shows that the state of Texas cares little for international law. Already, this violation has had international repercussions: Mexican President Vicente Fox has canceled his trip to Texas and his meeting with President Bush that were scheduled later this month.

Texas authorities did not advise Suarez of his right to contact his country's consulate when he was arrested, thus depriving him of the expert legal counsel that his government could provide. This is in violation of of Article 36 of the Vienna Convention, which the United States has signed.

This is not the first time, nor I suspect the last time, that Texas will ignore international law. Already, Texas has executed a number of foreign nationals whose rights under the Vienna Convention were violated. The state also has executed juvenile offenders (offenders who committed their crime before the age of 18) in violation of international law.

Atwood, a Houstonian, is a member of the Texas Coalition to Abolish the Death Penalty.

Texas should stop executing foreign nationals if it wants to be seen as a civilized state. But it should go further. It should also stop executing its own citizens. It should rise above an eye-for-an-eye mentality and demonstrate that killing is not the answer to killing.

This is not an easy thing to accomplish for people who have lost a loved one to murder. It is not easy for someone who believes that justice means getting even or settling the score. It is certainly not easy for politicians who believe that they must support the death penalty to get elected. But no one said that becoming a civilized state is easy. It takes time. It takes maturity. It takes wisdom.

It might be a different story if the death penalty were shown to be necessary for societal protection. However, in this day and age, society can be protected by long-term incarceration of dangerous criminals. Furthermore, all credible studies have shown that capital punishment has no deterrent effect. In fact, a survey of the nation's police chiefs indicated that they believe that capital punishment is the least effective measure to combat violent crime.

There are many "up sides" to seeking justice by means other than capital punishment. Several studies have shown that life in prison is less expensive than the death penalty. This is because of the huge legal costs involved with capital cases.

Secondly, the victim's family knows the outcome of the case early on. They do not have to wait years for someone to be executed and then find out that they did not get the "closure" they had been promised by prosecutors and victims' rights groups.

Thirdly, by not responding to killing with more killing, the state is setting a moral tone that is positive for all members of society. That is, killing is not justified under any circumstances. Life is truly sacred.

In its 2003 session, the Texas Legislature will have a number of opportunities to improve the criminal justice system of this state. By courageously outlawing capital punishment, the legislators will move Texas down the road toward becoming a truly civilized state.

Houston Chronicle, Aug. 16, 2002

Index of Names and Organizations

4th World Summit of Nobel Peace Laureates 21
5th U.S. Circuit Court of Appeals 32

A

Acosta, Rafael 14
Adams, Randall Dale 40, 43, 51
African Commission on Human and People's Rights 21
Africa for Life 21
Ageorges, Sandrine 22
Ahmed, Selina 15
Albright, Madeleine 18
Alito, Samuel 15
Allridge, James 63, 66, 68, 120
American Bar Association National Juvenile Defender Center 21
American Psychiatric Association 42
Amnesty International 7, 33, 37
Amore, Sister Jean 5
Andrea Pia Yates Support Coalition 38
ArtCar Museum 37
Atwood, Priscilla 1, 2, 19, 20, 21, 34, 62, 64, 66, 67, 74
Austin-American Statesman 51
Ayestas, Carlos 20

B

Bacci, Barbara 64, 66
Baird, Charles 31
Ballotta, Arianna 43, 116
Banks, Delma 40
Baptist General Convention of Texas 14
Barnes, Odell 45
Barnes, Roger C. v
Bass, Helen 45
Beazley, Napoleon 34, 59, 118
Beazley, Rena and Ireland 35
Benedictine monastery in Pecos, New Mexico 3
Biasio, Fabian 37, 48
Blackmun, Harry 33
Blank, Jessica 40

Bledsoe, Gary 51
Blom, Bishop Paul 14
Bonowitz, Abe 8
Boots, James and Lillian 59
Botean, John Michael 59
Brandley, Clarence 7, 34, 43, 51
Brooks, Charlie xi, 6
Brown, Gary 26
Brown, Lee 52
Burr, Dick 46
Bush, George W. xi, 14, 18, 19, 24, 25, 42, 56
Byars, Carol 25, 27
Byrd, James 21, 33
Byrd, Ross 21

C

Cahill, Tom 65
Cain, Darren 61
Cannon, Joe 57, 59, 68
Cantu, Ruben 46
Carabin, Joe 57
Carlson, Ronald 23, 25, 27
Carmody, Edmond 58
Carnahan, Mel 13
Carpenter, Pamela Moseley 50
Carter, Rubin "Hurricane" 17, 116
Catholic Bishops of Texas 12, 80
Catholic Campaign for Human Development xi, 3, 5
Catholic Herald 11
Chambers, Tony 36
Charlton, Mike 45
Cheatham, Ida 36
Cheever, Joan M. v
Chen, Martin 65
Chi, Heliberto 20
Chicago Tribune 47
Chirwa, Vera 17, 21
Cities for Life 20, 21
Citizens for Choice in Sentencing 50
Clenbennan, Brian 63
Clinton, Bill 19
Colburn, James 36, 37, 48
Collier, Rosalyn Falcón x
Congregation Or Ami 15
Cook, Kerry Max 40, 43, 51

Cornyn, John 32
Cruz, Oliver 68, 106
Cruz, Yolanda 60
Cushing, Renny 27

D

D'Elia, Sergio 21
Dallas Morning News 52, 53
Danziger, Richard 26
Davies, Nick 34
Dean, Jerry Lynn 23
DePriest, Nancy 26
DiNardo, Cardinal Daniel 62
Diocese of Galveston-Houston 12
Dold, Christa 63
Dominican Sisters of Houston, Texas 13, 86
Donnelly, Alan J. 98
Donovan, Kelly Elizabeth 59, 60
Dow, David 65
Drug Enforcement Agency 61
Dunbar, Tyrone 56
Dunne., Jimmy 119
Dutton, Harold 51, 52

E

Earle, Steve 58
Ekland-Olson, Sheldon 30
European Parliament 19
Evangelium Vitae 12

F

Farenthold, Frances (Sissy) iv
Farquhar, Kelly 58
Faulder, Joseph Stanley 17, 116
Ferguson, Cheryl 34
Fiorenza, Bishop Joseph A. 12, 65
Fox, Vincente 18
French Consulate 45
Fuentes, Anthony 67, 68

G

Garrett, Daniel 23
Garza, Juan 19
Ginsburg, Ruth Bader 31, 41
Gnavi, Marco 66
Gomez, Pedro 46
Gonzaga University 20
Gorbachev, Mikhail 21

Gough, Kathryn 66
Graham, Gary 7, 45, 59
Green, Dominique 20, 64, 68, 109
Grigson, James 41
Guerra, Ricardo Aldape 7, 40, 43
Gutierrez, Rachel 56

H

Hall, Chester Frank 56
Halperin, Dr. Rick 7
Hands Off Cain 19, 21
Harris, Dorothy Kaye 37
Hayslip, Denise 61
Henry, John Dale 56, 57
Holmes, Johnny 40
Hospitality House 44, 57
Houle, Kristin 36
Houston Chronicle 36, 46, 53
Hoyt, Kenneth M. 40

I

International Court of Justice 18
Italian Coalition to Abolish the Death Penalty 19, 116

J

Jaeger-Lane, Marietta 27
Jaggerstatter, Franz 106
Jensen, Eric 40
Johnson-Malley, Mitzi 58
Jones, Richard 43, 44
Journey of Hope...From Violence to Healing 8, 25
Justice for All 46

K

Kelly, Lorna 66
Kendall, George 40
Kilheffer, John 18
Klineberg, Steven 30
Ku Klux Klan 46

L

Lambert, Bobby 45
Landrum, Guy 67
Lastrapes, Andre 65, 109
Lastrapes, Andrew 65
Lastrapes, Bernatte 65, 109
Lawton, Stacey 35, 36

Livingston, Tammy 43
Lofthouse, Andrew 66
Long, Walter 21, 34, 35
Lopez, Richard 58
Lopez, Wanda Jean 47
Luna, Carlos De 47
Luttig, John E. 34

M

Maradiaga, Cardinal Oscar Andres Rodriguez 20
Marazziti, Mario iv, 21
Marino, Achim Josef 26
Marquart, James 30, 33
Marquez, Mario 56, 68
Marquez, Rebecca 56
McCarthy, The Reverend Emmanuel Charles 59, 103
McGinnis, Glen 55, 58, 68
McMillen, Carla 63
Mease, Darrel J. 13
Medellin, José Ernesto 18
Medina, Javiar 18
Meeker-Williams, Rev. Marilyn 14
Miller-El, Thomas 33
Mitchell, Gerald 59
Montoya, Irineo Tristan 18
Morris, Errol 40
Morris, Tina 37, 48
Murder Victims Families for Reconciliation 25, 38
Murphy, Judge Sheila 65
Murphy, Peggy 37
Murphy-Racey, Patrick 73

N

National Alliance on Mental Illness 39
National Association for the Advancement of Colored People 51
National Coalition to Abolish the Death Penalty 7, 8
National Conference of Black Mayors 51
Ndiaye, Bacre Waly 18, 92
Nobel Peace Laureates 21
Nobles, Jonathan 58, 68

O

O'Conner, Sandra Day 43
Oates, Louis 37
Ochoa, Christopher 26
Ogan, Craig 60, 68
Ortiz, Adam 21
Osadchey, Rabbi Shaul 15
Overstreet, Morris 31

P

Paneque, Santiaga 20
Panetti, Scott 38
Paroles, Texas Board of Pardons and 43
Patterson, Kelsey 36, 37, 43
Pattillo, Linda 59
Pax Christi 3
Pelke, Bill 8, 27, 63
Penalty, Texas Coalition to Abolish the Death xi
Penry, Johnny Paul 20, 50, 120
Perry, Governor Rick xi, 20, 37, 42, 43, 50, 65, 66
Phillips, Inez 17
Phillips, Scott 36
Pineda, Lastenia 20
Pope John Paul II 12, 13, 76
Popp, Jeanette 26, 27
Prejean, Sister Helen iv, 9, 20, 63, 117
Princeton University 2

R

Recinella, Dale 30
Rice, Thomas "Speedy" 20
Rice University 30
Riebschlaeger, Sister Elizabeth 14
Roberson, Brian 59, 68, 106
Roberts, John 15
Robison, Ken and Lois 36, 116
Robison, Larry 36
Rodenburg, Karl 58, 59
Rodriguez, Roger 62
Rosenthal, Chuck 38
Rothko Chapel 38
Ryan, George 51
Rytting, James 37

S

Sam Houston State University 26

Sankofa, Shaka 7, 45. *See* Graham, Gary
Sant' Egidio Community 20, 21, 22, 64, 66, 67
Santoro, Biagio 43
Sarandon, Susan 63
Scalia, Antonin 15
SHAPE Community Center 7
Sisters of Charity of the Incarnate Word 13, 87
Sorensen, Jonathan R. 30, 33
Southern Methodist University 7
Sparks, Sam 38, 43
Stein, Edith 106
Steven, John Paul 30

T

Tanksley, Jessica 66
Tate, Robert 67
Taylor, Gary 45
TCADP 18, 19, 21, 22, 37, 49, 52, 53. *See also* Texas Coalition to Abolish the Death Penalty
Texans Against State Killing March 7
Texas Board of Pardons and Paroles 24, 37, 42, 43, 45, 65, 66
Texas Coalition to Abolish the Death Penalty 7, 63, 67, 73. *See also* TCADP
Texas Conference of Churches 14, 88
Texas Court of Criminal Appeals 30, 32, 40, 51
Texas Defender Service 42, 63
Texas Democratic Party 52
Texas Fair Defense Act of 2001 32, 50
Texas Innocence Network 63, 65
Texas Moratorium Network 51
Texas Southern University 15
The Dallas Morning News 33
Thomas, Clarence 15
Thompson, Chuck 61
Thornton, Deborah 23
Tucker, Karla Faye 15, 20, 23, 25, 43, 115
Tutu, Archbishop Desmond 65

U

U.N. General Assembly 20
U.S. Catholic Bishops 6, 11, 12
U.S. Supreme Court 18, 32, 33, 35, 38, 40
United Methodist Church 14
United States Conference of Catholic Bishops 83
University of Denver 36
University of St. Thomas 65

V

Vienna Convention on Consular Relations 18, 20

W

Walsh, Ann 57
Walsh, Father Stephen 58, 61
Welch, Bud 27
Welch, Mandy 46
Westley, Anthony 56, 117
White, Ami 26, 27
White, George 8
White, Linda 26, 27
Wilkerson, Leta Ann 58
Willingham, Cameron Todd 47
Willis, Ernest 43
Wilson, Bishop Joe 14
World Coalition to Abolish the Death Penalty 21

Y

Yates, Andrea Pia 38

Z

Zelaya, Dennis 20

David Atwood is a retired petroleum industry engineer. Dave holds a BS degree from the University of Rochester and an MBA from New York University. He is the founder (1995) and past president of TCADP. He has been a member of the board since its founding. He has also been a member of the Board of Directors of the National Coalition to Abolish the Death Penalty and received their Lighting the Torch of Conscience Award. Dave has been involved in efforts to end the use of capital punishment for more than 15 years. He has been involved in issues of social justice for more than 20 years. He is the coordinator of Pax Christi Houston and has also served on the National Council of Pax Christi USA. Dave is a past president of the Houston Peace and Justice Center and served on the board as well. Dave resides in Houston, Texas. You can reach David at dpatwood@igc.org

Acknowledgements*

The San Antonio Peace Center, specifically Susan Ives and Rosalyn Collier, who have made this book possible.

"Texas Abolition Warriors" who have worked hard to abolish the death penalty in Texas: Dr. Rick Halperin, Susybelle Gosslee, Dr. Roger Barnes, Joan Cheever, Marta Glass, Nancy Bailey, Tom Keene, Johnny Martinez, Jim and Sherry Coombes, Bob and Jean Van Steenburg, Adele Marks, Marj Loehlin, Rich Woodward, Carole Johnson, Alison Dieter, Delia Meyer, Vicki McCuistion, Kristin Houle, Jeanne Adams, Curt Crum, Vince Gonzales, Jesse Doiron, Robert Gazaway, Wayne Daniel, Rev. Wanda Ritchea, Emily Cheatham, Stan Allridge, Burnham and Joan Terrell, Regina Schmahl, Pat Nichols, Lynn Furay, Angie Agapetus, Barbara Acuna, Sherri Clausell, Gloria Rubac, Joann Gavin, Njeri Shakur, Massoud and Debbie Nayeri, Lee Greenwood, Guy and Ursula Landrum, Scott Cobb, Bryan McCann, Stefanie Collins, Lily Hughes, Michael Corwin, Dana Cloud, James Moore, Dennis Longmire, Kelly Epstein, Shirley Farrell, Sylvia Garza, John Sullivan, Ida Cheatham, Mike Kennedy (deceased), Carol Tures, Ricky and Sharon Jason, Deloyd Parker, Minister Robert Muhammad, Steve Hall, Ken and Lois Robison, Ward Larkin, Hooman Hedayati, Karen Sebung, Lawrence Foster, Amy O'Sullivan, Rena and Ireland Beazley, Yolanda Cruz, Bill Vaught, Jimmy Dunne, Katy Feyh, Nicole Horne, Casey Davis, Joy Weathers.

"National Abolition Warriors" who have helped us here in Texas: Sr. Helen Prejean, Sr. Jean Amore, Susan Sarandon, Danny Glover, Abe Bonowitz, Diann Rust-Tierney, David Elliott, Steve Hawkins, Shari Silberstein, Mike Farrell, Governor George Ryan, Martin Luther King III, Dick Gregory, Richard Dieter, Andre Latallade, Kurt Rosenberg, Claudia Whitman, Betsy Fairbanks, Michael Radelet, Magdaleno Rose Avila, Rachel King, Sue Gunawardena-Vaughn, Kathy Harris

"International Abolition Warriors" who have helped us here in Texas: Arianna Ballotta and Biagio Santoro, Michela and Carlo Mancini, Chiara Silva , Barbara Bacci, Mario Marazziti, Carlo Santoro, Gianni Giudotti,, Fr. Marco Gnavi, Stefania Tallei, Sandrine Ageorges, Marjan Cochez, Karl Rodenberg , Sergio D'Elia, Katia Rabbachi and many, many others.

Family Members of Murder Victims who have spoken out strongly against the death penalty in Texas: Linda and Ami White, Carol Byars (deceased), Ron Carlson, Jeanette Popp, Robert Hoelscher, Ross Byrd, Bernatte Lastrapes, Andre and Andrew Lastrapes, Bill Pelke, George White, SueZann Bosler, Marietta Jaeger-Lane, Bud Welch, Celia McWee and many, many others.

Exonerated Prisoners who have spoken out strongly against the death penalty in Texas: Randall Dale Adams, Kerry Max Cook, Clarence Brandley, Shujaa Graham, Ray Krone, Ron Kiene, Juan Melendez, Greg Wilhoit, and others.

Members of the Faith Community who have been strong supporters: Sr. Margaret Bulmer, Sr. Benedict Shannon, Sr. Jane Abell, Sr. Ceil Roeger, Sr. Elizabeth Riebschlaeger, Sr. Barbara Netek, Sr. Mildred Truchard, Sr. Claude Demoustier, Sr. Kathleen Judge, Pope John Paul II, Catholic Bishops of Texas (especially Archbishop Joseph Fiorenza), Bishop Joe Wilson, Bishop Paul Blom, Bishop Walter Sullivan, Andy Rivas, Br. Richard Daly, Fr. Richard Wahl, Fr. John Robbins, Fr. John Lasseigne, Fr. Gerry Kelly, Deacon Harry Davis, Deacon Al O'Brien, Deacon Michael Liebrecht, Deacon Sam Dunning, Jim Barrette, Rev. Carroll Pickett, Rabbi Shaul Osadchey, Rev. Marilyn Meeker-Williams, Rev. Bruce Felker., Sr. Martha Ann Kirk, Fr. John Manion.

Defense Attorneys who have worked hard to defend death row prisoners and improve the criminal justice system: David Dow, Andrea Keilen, Jared Tyler, Jim Marcus, Keith Hampton, Walter Long, George Parnham, Maurie Levin, Gregory Wiercioch, Morris Moon, Kathryn Kase, Dana Lynn Recer, Rob Owen, John Niland, Nicole Casarez, Paul Nugent, Mike DeGeurin, Pat McCann, John Wright, Dick Burr, Mandy Welch.

Texas Criminal Court of Appeals Judges who have worked hard to bring justice to Texas: Charley Baird, Morris Overstreet

District Attorneys who have spoken out for justice in Texas: Sam Millsap, Craig Watkins

Legislators for Justice and Life: Sen. Rodney Ellis, Sen. Juan Hinojosa, Sen. Eliott Shapleigh, Sen. Eddie Lucio, Jr., Rep. Harold Dutton, Rep. Dora Olivo, Rep. Elliott Naishtat, Rep. Terri Hodge, Rep. Lon Burnham, Rep. Ellen Cohen, Rep. Garnet Coleman, Rep. Jessica Farrar, Rep. Senfronia Thompson.

Organizations who have worked against the death penalty in Texas: ACLU of Texas, Amnesty International, Campaign to End the Death Penalty, Dallas Peace Center, Harris County Green Party, Houston Peace and Justice Center, Pax Christi Texas, SHAPE Community Center, StandDown Project, Texas Civil Right Project, Texas Death Penalty Abolition Movement, Texas Moratorium Network, Texas Students to Abolish the Death Penalty, Journey of Hope...From Violence to Healing, Witness to Innocence, Equal Justice USA, Murder Victims Families for Reconciliation, Murder Victims Families for Human Rights, National Coalition to Abolish the

Death Penalty, Catholic Church, United Methodist Church, Unitarian Universalists, Quakers, Dominican Sisters of Houston, Sisters of Charity of the Incarnate Word, Maryknoll Fathers and Brothers, Basilean Fathers.

Other Supporters of our work to abolish the death penalty in Texas: Judge Sheila Murphy, Sissy Farenthold, Thomas Cahill, Les Breeding, James Harrington, Adam Axel, Professor Selina Ahmed, Greg Audel, Patrick Spedale, Tommy Calais, Anne Doyle, Jenny McConnell, Karen and Guy Clifton, Barbara Budde, Alicia Alvarez, Joyce and Mac Hall, Frank Skeith, Ellen Burns, Cathie and Tico Foley, Joe and Laura Marcinowski, Stephanie Weber, Ellie Collier, Eileen Dolan, Elizabeth Jeter, Tom Lawrence, Ada Edwards, Jew Don Boney, Jolanda Jones, Connie Nash, Bill and Cheryl Crosier, Ann Geyer, Billy and Jodie Sinclair, Brian Evans, Phivan Wright, Michael Skadden, Courtney Wilson, Lee Loe, Jac Battiste, Rob Block, Gislaine Williams, Nick Cooper, Renee Feltz, Ray Hill, P.K. McCary, Wally James, Hitaji Aziz, Art Browning, Christine Morshedi, Danny Yeager, Deborah Bell, Rick Doucette, Ester King, Prof. Trish Vandiver, Prof. John Burke, Prof. Bob Buzzanco, Ernest McMillan, Steve Mills, Michael Possley, Jim Harithas, Ralph McCloud, Sophia Malik, Tina Morris, Sue Ann Lorig, Scott Poteet, David and Maribel Gerling, Dr. Wayne Shandera, Maria Jiminez, Patsy Cravens, Paola Pizzitoli, Craig Washington, Brigitta Knickenberg.

Artists/Photographers/Filmmakers/Musicians who have supported our abolition work in Texas: Sara Hickman, Shelley Shanks, Jude Thetford, Rafael Acosta, Ken Light, Barbara Sloan, Fabian Biasio, Micki Dickoff, Steve James, Peter Gilbert, Rickey Jason, Charlie King, Karen Brandow, Nanci Griffith, Steve Earle, Capital "X"

Radio/Media Support: KPFT Radio Houston, Houston Indymedia, Greenwatch, KDOL Radio,

Newspaper Support: Dallas Morning News, Austin American Statesman, Houston Chronicle, San Antonio Express-News, Ft. Worth Star Telegram, Austin Chronicle, Texas Observer, Dallas Observer, Houston Peace News, The Touchstone, Texas Catholic Herald, Chicago Tribune

* This is a list of people and organizations that I am familiar with and can recall. Undoubtedly there are many more that I have failed to list. I apologize to those people and organizations that have been inadvertently left out.

Texas Coalition to Abolish the Death Penalty

The Texas Coalition to Abolish the Death Penalty (TCADP) is a statewide, grassroots organization comprised of individuals and groups who work to end the death penalty through education and action. We are a non-profit organization with 501(c)((3)) status. Donations are tax deductible. We invite you to join the TCADP today. You will receive the TCADP newsletter when you join.

___ $100 Sustaining Donation

___ $50 Annual Joint Donation

___ $30 Annual Donation

___ $15 Student/Fixed Income

___ Enclosed is an additional tax deductible contribution of $_____ to support the work of the TCADP.

Please mail to: TCADP, 2709 S. Lamar Blvd., Austin, TX 78704.

Name: _____

Address: _____

_____
      City   State   Zip

Phone - Home: _____

       - Work _____

       - Cell: _____

E-Mail: _____

Newsletter: ___ print or ___ e-mail

All information will be kept in strictist confidence.

Contributions can also be made online through the TCADP website: www.tcadp.org

To contact the TCADP, call (512) 441-1808 or email info@tcadp.org.

About peaceCENTER Books

Since 2007, the San Antonio peaceCENTER has been conducting an experiment in community-based publishing, distributing time-tested information written from decades of collective grassroots experience, designed for all who seek peace, teach peace, demonstrate peace and celebrate peace.

Detour to Death Row by David Atwood, founder, Texas Coalition to Abolish the Death Penalty

Facilitator's Manual for the Class of Nonviolence, by Susan Ives, with a foreword by Colman Mccarthy

Hajj Journal, by Narjis Pierre, with an introduction and photographs by Ali Moshirsadri

Insights on the Journey: *Trauma, Healing and Wholeness.* An Anthology of Women's writing compiled by Maureen Leach, OSF

Peace is Our Birthright: *the p.e.a.c.e. process and interfaith community development* by Ann E. Helmke and Rosalyn Falcón Collier, with a foreword by Arun Gandhi

Working It Out! *Managing and Mediating Everyday Conflicts* by Rosalyn Falcón Collier

Books are available for purchase from the peaceCENTER Web site, www.salsa.net/peace/ebooks, in two formats:
• Convenient and affordable eBooks (downloadable Adobe Acrobat files)
• Trade paperbacks (available for purchase from Amazon.com)

Please contact the peaceCENTER for information about bulk discounts for activists, classes, community organizations and book stores.

Profits generated by peaceCENTER books support the work of the peaceCENTER and its peacePARTNERS.

"Wherever they burn books they will also, in the end, burn human beings."
Heinrich Heine

Focused on the vision of Peace in our lives,
the interfaith peaceCENTER supports
the learning of peace through prayer and
education; and supports the demonstration
of peace through nonviolent actions
and community.
The peaceCENTER is a 501(c)(3) nonprofit organization

1443 S. St. Mary's San Antonio, TX 78210
210.224.HOPE   www.salsa.net/peace
pcebooks@yahoo.com

3149850

Made in the USA